Fifty
Difficult Passages
Explained

by
Jay E. Adams

TIMELESS TEXTS
Stanley, North Carolina

Bible quotations are from:

The Christian Counselor's New Testament and Proverbs, TIMELESS TEXTS, Stanley, NC, © 1977, 1980, 1994, 2000 by Jay E. Adams.

The *NEW AMERICAN STANDARD BIBLE*, © 1960, 1962, 1963, 1968, 1971, 1972, 1973, 1975, 1977, 1995 by The Lockman Foundation. Used by permission.

The *King James Version* of the Bible.

© 2008 by Jay E. Adams
ISBN: 978-1-889032-64-1

All Rights Reserved

Printed in the United States of America

CONTENTS

INTRODUCTION

It's not that the passages that I consider in this book are actually difficult, in and of themselves. It is because of the failure to translate properly, the outmoded language in translations, traditional misunderstandings, cultural differences, and matters of that sort, that they are difficult *to us*. Because many sincere Christians struggle to interpret them, because others misinterpret them, and because still others give up trying to interpret them, I have decided to offer this book as a help.

Now, I understand that some will disagree with my interpretations; that, of course, is their privilege. When they do, I hope that they will do so out of careful study and for serious exegetical reasons – not merely because they do not like my explanations or because these explanations may differ from their theology. The purpose of this book, as I said, is to offer help to those who are truly seeking help, not to push various views or to stir up controversy. Where people rightly may differ, however, there is likely to be some controversy. That is not always bad, so long as the dialog grows out of and maintains exegetical concerns. Controversy of that sort can only lead to greater understanding.

I do not claim that all of my explanations of the passages presented are original. Indeed, if they were, you would have reason to suspect what I have to say. No one person has the corner on truth. However, even when there are interpretations that have been offered by others, often these are not accessible to all, since they may be couched in scholarly jargon. I have become known for simplifying complex matters, and in such cases my hope is to write in ways that most Christians can understand.

The choice of passages was made purely out of my own observations that they needed explanation to many Christians. I have spent years holding conferences all over the country and around the world, I have taught in two theological seminaries, and lectured in any number of others, and I have pastored several congregations. Having thus acquired a rather broad outlook during my 79 years, I think that I am acquainted with passages that are commonly misunderstood.

At any rate, for what value it may have, I send forth this volume with the profound hope that it will contribute to some extent in bringing about a time when the Bible will be better understood by larger numbers, so that the great truths about our Lord Jesus Christ that it reveals may be comprehended more fully and, as a consequence, the blessings of those truths may be extended to many.

Jay Adams, 2008
Enoree, SC

GENESIS 2:17

"in the day that you eat from it
you will surely die."

...but from the tree of the knowledge of good
and evil you shall not eat, for in the day that
you eat from it you shall surely die.

But *did* Adam die? Of course, we read about his living
until the age of eight hundred years after begetting Seth
(Genesis 5:4). Obviously, therefore, Moses himself tells us
that he did not die "in the day" that he ate of the forbidden
fruit. Does that mean Moses contradicted himself? Did he
misrepresent God in saying that Adam would die immediately after eating of the fruit? How can we understand this?

The devil was not right when he told Eve, "you will not
die" (Genesis 3:4). God was right, and Moses was right too.
The fact is, as the New Testament unmistakably tells us, there
is more than one kind of death. And Paul explains very
plainly that "death reigned from Adam to Moses" (Romans
5:14), and that "death reigned because of one person's tres-
pass" (Romans 5:17). He was speaking of *spiritual* death.
Physically, Adam lived on; spiritually, he died the moment he
disobeyed God.

Death is separation. Physical death is the separation of the
spirit from the body (James 2:26). Similarly, spiritual death is
separation – the separation of the spirit from God. He who
walked with God in the cool of the day prior to his disobedience, hid from Him afterwards. Their close union had been
disrupted. Eternal death is the separation of the spirit and
body from God forever.

Similarly, life is union: physical life is the union of the
body and spirit, spiritual life is the union of the spirit with
God through Christ, and eternal life is the union of the body
and the spirit with God for all eternity.

So, there is no question about it: death that subsequently
"reigned from Adam to Moses" began immediately upon

3

Adam's act of disobedience. It is also true that from that day on man began the process of deterioration (corruption) that inevitably leads to physical death. The Bible is not wrong; it is the materialistic literalist, who fails to see the greater spiritual consequences of one's relationship to God, who is wrong.

GENESIS 2:24

"and the two shall become one flesh"

For this reason a man shall leave his father and mother, and be joined to his wife; and they shall become one flesh.

"Well, what's difficult about this passage? Doesn't it say that two people shall be joined together and shall have sex?" Well, no, on several counts. First, it says a man and a wife are joined together, not merely two people. There are those who try to call a same sex relationship a marriage. That simply doesn't fit the biblical model. God's Word is explicit about that.

But second, it does say that a man and a wife are joined together in marriage. That verb joined (literally, "glued") together speaks of a *permanent* relationship. Not a trial relationship that, if it doesn't work out, may be terminated. Jesus said, "What God has yoked together, a human being must not separate" (Matthew 19:6). So, divorce, though allowed for unrepentant adultery and desertion, was not in view in Genesis 2. The goal was to cement a permanent relationship between a man and his wife.

But neither does the passage speak about sexual relations. The words "one flesh" have a different meaning. The word "flesh," in Hebrew, had much the same meaning as our word "body." They, like us, used the word to mean "person." When we say "everybody," we do not think of every *body* (as though we were speaking only of meat and bones). Rather we think of every *person*. So, too when the Hebrew wrote "all flesh" it meant all persons, or everybody. Just a few chapters later, for instance, when Moses was foretelling the flood to come, He said, "God looked on the earth, and behold, it was corrupt; for all flesh had corrupted their way upon the earth" (Genesis 6:11). Joel wrote that God would pour out His Spirit on "all flesh" (Joel 2:28; i.e., upon all sorts of persons). So, the two becoming one flesh meant that they were to become so close that they would function like one person. Of course, the fall of man has kept the marriage relationship from measuring up to that ideal. Men and women, apart from salvation and sanctification, do not even begin to approach such unity of companionship. Yet, in Christ, they can learn to approach it more and more.

GENESIS 4:6, 7

"If you do well, will you not be accepted?"

> Then the Lord said to Cain, "Why are you
> angry? And why has your countenance fallen?
> If you do well, won't your countenance be
> lifted up? And if you don't do well, sin is
> crouching at the door, and its desire is for you,
> but you must master it."

This seems to teach salvation by works, but it doesn't. The
second, more accurate translation, makes that clear. But what
is the passage all about? It is an account of a very gracious act
of God toward Cain that was rejected. Cain was angry because
God had accepted Abel's offering and not his own (Genesis
4:3–5). This He did not because one was a bloody offering and
the other was not. The passage makes no such point. Each
man offered something that pertained to his own work. The
notion about a bloody sacrifice is read back into these verses
by interpreters.

Well, then, what does the passage say about the two offer-
ings? It says that Abel gave of the *first and the fat (best)* of
his flock as an offering to God. But about Cain it says that, *in
time*, he gave an offering. The point of the passage is that one
gave the first and the best; the other simply gave something
without regard to whether it was the first and the best. It was
on that basis that one offering was accepted and the other
rejected.

Cain became angry at his brother because his offering was
accepted rather than his own. Then Lord then came to Cain
and spoke the words of the verses before us. He first alerted
Cain to the fact that his anger against his brother had no
basis. He then warned him that if he didn't straighten up and
do those things he knew were right, his anger would lead to
greater sin.

Incidentally, the fact that one's sin leads to a dejected face,
and that his countenance will be lifted up only when he

begins to obey and please God, is an important fact for all biblical counselors and for their counselees. There is no good reason for anger and dejection when one has brought his problems on himself. Depression can be dispelled by repenting of sin and doing those things that one ought to have done in the first place.

Moreover, sin, not dealt with in repentance, may lead to far greater sin. When one is depressed, angry and dejected, he is vulnerable to additional sin. It creeps up and then crouches at his door like an animal, ready to spring upon him. Cain failed to heed God's gracious warning and went on to slay his brother. Sin, early on in human history, led to death; the first man born to Adam and Eve became a murderer!

So, the King James Version, which has "accepted" rather than "lifted up" in verse 7 leads the reader astray. It is not that *Cain* would be accepted by doing right, but that his *countenance* would be lifted up. His dejection, depression and anger would dissipate only when he began to do the right things.

GENESIS 4:17

"Cain had relations with his wife..."

Cain had relations with his wife and she conceived, and gave birth to Enoch.

One of the old saws is that the Bible is incorrect because it says that Cain had a wife when there was no one for him to marry. The question, "Where did Cain get his wife?" is as old as is Bible criticism. But the answer is just as old – or older! Yet, in spite of that fact, the question is still bandied about. So, it is important to mention that answer for any who might be perplexed.

Obviously, Cain and Abel were not the only children of Adam. That Adam and Eve had other children besides Cain and Abel is straightforwardly stated in Genesis 5:4 "Then the days of Adam after he became the father of Seth were eight hundred years, *and he had other sons and daughters.*" The answer is that simple! Cain and Abel are prominent because of the incidents recorded with reference to their relationship, which ended in the tragic death of Abel. The importance of mentioning Cain is also to show how soon the effects of sin began to manifest themselves – the first man born was a murderer! The human race has been corrupt from the outset. Until the coming of Jesus Christ, only Adam and Eve had been sinless; and they sinned and brought sin into humanity.

It is clear that Cain must have married one of his sisters. That there would be few deleterious genetic problems that early in the history of mankind seems probable, so that there would be no reason why Cain should not marry one of his siblings. At any rate, since there were no other women around to marry, it seems certain that this was what happened.

EXODUS 20:13

"Thou shalt not kill."

You must not murder.

How is it that God commanded men not to kill and then also commanded the sacrifice of thousands of animals? How is it that He called upon His people to exterminate the people dwelling in the land of Palestine, if they were not to kill? Those questions, in one form or another, are regularly asked by people who are not very familiar with the Bible, but who at least know something of the ten commandments and the history of Israel.

The question is answered very simply. The word translated "kill" in the King James Version is not the word for killing in general. Rather, it is the word for *murder*: "You must not murder." To kill, in the instances mentioned above (as well as in others) is not murder.

Those who use Exodus 20:13 to advocate vegetarianism or pacifism *mis*use the verse. This, like many other problems that we have to deal with as the result of faulty translations, is a difficulty of the church's own making. Not only has the church usually set forth the ten commandments in the King James Version, but it has taught several generations to memorize them in the words of that version. It is time that we started using a more accurate translation so that people will no longer be confused by it. Traditionalism is hard to counter.

EXODUS 21:11

"And if he will not do these three things for her,
then she shall go out for nothing,
without payment of money."

> If he takes to himself another, he may not
> diminish her food, her clothing or her conjugal
> rights. And if he will not do these three things
> for her, then she shall go out for nothing, with-
> out the payment of money.

Understand the picture presented in the passage. Out of
poverty one sells his daughter as a maid-servant who becomes
recognized as a wife or concubine (v. 7). If, for some reason,
the new husband seriously neglects to do the duties of a husband (designated by the three things mentioned in v. 11), she
is allowed to leave him without the monetary payment of
redemption that was otherwise required to free her (as mentioned in v. 8). What impact does this have on the church?
The interesting passage provides some help in the matter of
determining when a divorce is legitimate in our day.

The passage clearly lists "three" elements that are so basic
to marriage that if all three cease to be a part of the marriage
relationship, this fact allows for the separation of the wife
from her husband. She is no longer "bound" (I Corinthians
7:15). They are provision of food, clothing (or shelter), and
sexual relations.

There are circumstances in which there is a question
whether or not a marriage has so deteriorated that it is possible to declare that the husband has "abandoned" his wife,
even when he has not done so *physically*. He has remained in
the house, but he has so neglected these three duties – which
here are set forth as the three basic elements constituting a
valid marriage – that he may no longer lay claim to his wife as
a wife. Counselors, and others who are concerned about the

situation in which they find such conditions persisting should take this passage into consideration.

But, you say, this was true in the state of polygamy; that is not our situation in America today. But think: if a *polygamist* was required to faithfully discharge these three duties, how much more so should a monogamist? Should he be allowed to treat his one wife more severely than one was allowed to treat a polygamist wife in OT times?

The church, of course, should first rebuke a member for so neglecting his wife. And, if necessary, it should bring discipline to cause him to repent. In such cases, if the discipline is successful, and the man shows the fruit of his repentance by faithfully resuming his obligations to his wife, there is no cause for her to leave him. But if he refuses, and is put out of the church for that refusal (as he should be), then he falls into the category of a "Gentile and a tax-collector" (Matthew 18:17).[1] As such, he is outside the authority and the discipline of the church, and, as I Corinthians 7:15 states, the sister is no longer subject to the marriage bonds. She may divorce ("go out from" him; cf. Deuteronomy 24:2).

This passage in Exodus should be understood in relationship to the many other passages that relate to divorce and remarriage. For information on how they do so, see my book, *Marriage, Divorce and Remarriage in the Bible.*

---

1. Cf. I Timothy 5:8 where a man who refuses to provide for his own is said to be worse than an unbeliever.

NUMBERS 23:19; GENESIS 6:6

"It repenteth the Lord..."

God is not a man...that He should repent.

"Well, does God repent or doesn't He? Is there a contradiction or isn't there?" No, God does not repent and no, there isn't a contradiction. That words could not be more plain than in these two verses, I will grant you. In Numbers, we are told that God does not repent; in Genesis we are told that He did. How can these words be explained – or *can* they?

The explanation is quite simple, but very important because it pertains to many other passages as well. In Genesis, we are dealing with anthropomorphic language; in Numbers, straightforward language.

Numbers is speaking about the very nature of God Himself. He is being compared to human beings who change their minds, who are sorry for decisions that they have made. They repent. But God, we are assured, is not like that: "He is not a man that He should repent." From all eternity He has decreed whatever comes to pass. It is certain. Because of that fact we can be sure of His prophecies and His promises. If He were like a man – changing His mind at will – then nothing in the universe would be certain. That is what Numbers tells us.

But what of Genesis? That is where anthropomorphism comes into play., The word comes from two Greek terms that mean "man" and "form." As applied to God, the word means that at times He speaks to us or is represented to us *as if* He were a man. He is pictured in man's form. We read of God's arm, His eye, etc. But these passages tell us nothing about His being. Actually, He has no body; He is pure Spirit (John 4:24). So when we read that God "repents" the passage is speaking as if He were acting like a man.

But why does God speak in this manner? He does so in order to help us understand something about ourselves. Men upon the earth had grown so wicked that (if God were a man) it would be *as if* He were to say about us, "I regret making you!" He speaks in our language to get a point across.

God not only talks about Himself as if He were human; elsewhere, for similar reasons, He talks as if He were an animal or an inanimate object. We read that we may rest under the shadow of His wings. God is not a cosmic chicken! He is represented as providing the protection, warmth and care that a bird gives to her chicks. He is called a "rock" and a "fortress" in order to stress His ability and desire to protect us from harm. So, when God wants to convey some attitude or other thought to us, He will often speak as if He were a man.

In contrast to all such anthropomorphic passages, the verse in Numbers is telling us what God is actually like in His very being. There, no figure of speech comes into play. The language is straightforward – it says that God, *as the divine being that He is*, does not change His mind. He is not sorry He made man;[1] He is never sorry for anything He ever did. In Genesis, when telling us how bad our sin is, He speaks as if He were a man, regretting the fact that He made us. But, as God, of course He has no regrets.

---

1. Cf. My book *The Grand Demonstration* for reasons why God is glad that He made man.

PSALM 2:2

"The kings of the earth take their stand,
and the rulers take counsel together
against the Lord and against His Anointed."

> The kings of the earth take their stand, and the
> rulers take counsel together against the Lord
> and His Anointed: "Let us tear their fetters
> apart, and cast away their cords from us!"

Was this prediction fulfilled? Is it yet future, as some suppose? Have the kings of the earth risen up in rebellion as the passage indicates? There should be no question about it. In the prayer found in Acts 4:24 and following, there is a clear reference to Psalm 2, in which the "gathering together" of "Herod and Pontius Pilate" with "the Gentiles and the people of Israel against" Jesus is said to be the fulfillment of the prophecy.

The reason it is important to recognize that the second Psalm had its fulfillment in Jesus' time is that the language to some seems more grandiose than the events that happened. The "Gentiles raging" (Acts 4:25), for instance, makes some think of great upheavals among nations. But the fulfillment in the eyes of the inspired apostles seemed grand, not because of the magnitude of the physical or political activities that occurred, but because of their spiritual significance.

This fact ought to give caution to some who interpret prophecy in a manner that would call for a literal or far more extensive fulfillment than was the intention of the prophet. The death, the ascension, and the seating of the Messiah on the throne of God was, of course, a magnificent heavenly event. It, too, is recorded in the same Psalm (vv. 4–12).

The granting of universal possession of the "nations" to Jesus Christ, extending to the very "ends of the earth" (Psalm 2:8 and Matthew 28:19, 20), seems impossible to many because they fail to recognize that Psalm 2:6–8 is the basis of the Great Commission in Matthew 28:19.

So we see that Acts 4:25–26 enables us to interpret Psalm 2:2. This principle, of using the New Testament to interpret the Old, can guide us in interpreting other passages as well. (See also Acts 13:32, 33 and Hebrews 1:5; 5:5 for other examples of New Testament passages that help us interpret this particular Psalm.)

PSALM 34:9

"O fear the Lord, you His saints;
for to those who fear Him, there is no want"

> O fear the Lord, you His saints; for to those
> who fear Him, there is no want...Come, you
> children, listen to me; I will teach you the fear
> of the Lord.

Many wonder about the expression "to fear the Lord," one that runs throughout the Bible and plays an important role in much of it. Does it mean dread or reverence? Or is there some other thought in it? One of the significant things here (and in other places) is that it takes on a quasi-technical sense. Clearly it means more than emotion. Indeed, in this passage we are told that one person can *teach* another to fear the Lord. Emotions cannot be taught.

So to what does the expression refer? In the Psalm before us we are given more than a hint. Some of the components are set forth. In verse 12, we are told that it is for the one who "desires life" and "loves length of days." And we further are informed that it consists of keeping one's "tongue from evil" and his "lips from speaking deceit" (v. 13). In addition, the writer says that the fear of the Lord involves "depart[ing] from evil and do[ing] good"; "seek[ing] peace and pursu[ing] it" (v. 14). Clearly, two things stand out in this description: 1) that these are but samples of the sort of thing that fearing the Lord is all about and 2) that the fear of the Lord is *a way of life*. It is, in fact, what we may call today "the Christian life." That is the way in which Peter seems to think of it in I Peter 3, where he quotes much of the passage.

So, to teach the fear of the Lord is to teach God's revealed way of life in which, it will be right to say, one lives out of respect for Him and in fear of the consequences of not doing so. This worthy biblical expression ought to be more widely used today and its meaning should be explained.

PSALM 51:4

"Against You and You only I have sinned"

Against You, and You only, I have sinned, and
done what is evil in Your sight, so that You are
justified when you speak, and blameless when
You judge.

Didn't David sin against Bathsheba and Uriah her husband? How, then, could he write these words? They seem to say that he considered his sin against God alone. Many have wondered about this; it is time to straighten the matter out.

First, there are those who think that it is improper to say that sin is against anyone but God alone. But that could not be correct, since Jesus represents the prodigal son as saying that he sinned against His father as well as against heaven.[1]

The explanation of the expression in question seems to be found in II Samuel 12:12, 13 where we read what the Lord said to David about his sin. He said: "Indeed you did it secretly, but I will do this thing before all Israel, and under the sun" (v. 12). The words "this thing" refer back to the calamities mentioned in verses 10 and 11, that would follow his sin. He would be involved in war the rest of his days, and in the future great trouble would plague his household.

It is important to note what God then points out to David: "Indeed, you did it *secretly.*" David acted in secret, where God alone could see him. In contrast, God promised to show his disapproval of David's sin, and of his covering it up, by making His response widely known. This prophecy came true not only in David's time, but in all time since – wherever the Bible is read. David tried to hide his sin from all but God, but God would not hide His response to it.

In response to the Lord's words spoken by Nathan the

---

1. "Heaven" is a common way of speaking of God. It is like saying "The White House said" when one means that its principal occupant was the one who said it.

prophet, David said: "I have sinned against the Lord" (v. 13). Upon confession of his sin, Nathan declared him forgiven (v. 13), but said that his child would die (v. 14). Why, if David had been forgiven? After forgiveness, there are often consequences that must result. God took the life of the baby born from the illicit union because, as He said, "...you have given occasion to the enemies of the Lord to blaspheme" (v. 14). He would not allow others to think that sin could be done and no consequences follow.

Now, consider once again Psalm 51:4. David speaks of doing what he did in God's sight alone. What he meant was that he had covered it up for a long time so that God alone knew what he had done. The phrase translated "against you" is more accurately translated "to you" or "before you." David understood that his sin had been committed "before," or in the sight of, God. What he hid from others, until Nathan confronted him, was done in the sight of God alone. David referred to this hiding of his sin as "silence" in Psalm 32:3, where he details the miseries of failing to confess it.

Even though others might have wondered about God's actions toward David prior to his psalms of penitence, David affirms now that he understands that what God did to him was just and blameless. So, in consequence of Nathan's confrontation, what had been hidden was now coming to the fore. What David and God alone had known (v. 3), would now become public knowledge. People would even sing psalms of confession based upon his sin, his hiding of it, his final confession and God's gracious forgiveness.

The great lesson to learn – that David himself wishes to teach through these penitential psalms (cf. Psalm 51:13) – is to quickly repent and confess sin rather than having to be forced to confess like a stubborn horse or mule that has to be dragged by his bit into submission (Psalm 32:9). The hiding of sin, and the fact that David thought he could keep his sin silent, is one of the principal messages of the psalms we are considering. To understand Psalm 51:4, therefore, is to understand a key to that message.

PROVERBS 23:6, 7

"As a man thinketh in his heart, so is he"

> Don't eat a stingy man's food, and don't desire
> his delicacies, since he is really what he thinks
> in himself. Though he say to you "Eat, drink,"
> his heart isn't with you.

Some who depend solely upon the words of the King
James Version for an understanding of verse 7 turn it into a
philosophy of life: "As a man thinketh in his heart, so is he."
In this version, these words seem to set forth a principle
intended to be applicable to all of life. Moreover, these interpreters fail to recognize that, unlike some of the earlier chapters of Proverbs, verse 7a occurs in a *context* (vv. 6–8). This
context, once understood, dissolves the idea that there is a
larger principle being set forth.[1] Let us look at the context to
see what it is that the writer had in mind.

First, consider verse 6: "Don't eat a stingy man's food, and
don't desire his delicacies." That is the background against
which the word about thinking in the heart is set. The concern in the verse is to warn the reader against letting one's
appetite ("desire" for food) rule when one is invited to eat at
the table of a stingy man. The passage is saying, "Think about
something more than how good it looks and how much you'd
like to eat a lot of it. He may say to you 'Eat, drink,' as though
you were welcome to all you could possibly want (v. 7), but
you must not take his words at face value. Consider what he is
really thinking within himself – in his heart."

Inwardly, the stingy man who is urging more food on you
will probably be thinking something like this: "I hope the pig
doesn't take that second pork chop [to give it a N.T. era appli-

---

1. That is not to say that one could not deduce a principle from the passage
if used in conjunction with some of the New Testament passages that have
to do with the heart. Surely, the word here correlates nicely with such passages. But the intent of Proverbs 23:7ᵃ is lost if it is merely turned into
some sort of general principle.

cation!]; I want it for myself for tomorrow."[1] His "heart (real intention) is not with you." That is, he says one thing but he means another. He may be speaking politely, but what he says isn't what he wants you to do. So, "don't eat" that extra helping. Consider that not everything one says is what he really means, and refrain.

If you do indulge yourself without thinking, you will regret having done so later on: "the bit you have eaten you will vomit up and lose your compliments." When you find out – too late – that he didn't mean what he said, you will feel like *vomiting up* what you have eaten and taking back the *compliments* that you wasted on him for his seeming generosity. That is the intent of the passage.

It is possible that verses 1 through 3, which speak about eating a ruler's food may also play into the interpretation of verses 6–8. But the passages may be in close juxtaposition merely because they both speak of restraint at the table. The guest's consideration should lead him to "put a knife" to his throat if he has "a hearty appetite[2]" (vv. 1, 2). Why? Because the ruler's "delicacies" are "deceitful food." That is to say, they are placed there as a test to determine what one will do when presented with a table full of food. The king sets out a lavish meal for his guests in order to learn something about them. He may wine and dine them to discover something of their manners and self-restraint. Perhaps he is considering whom to choose for a sensitive post. He wants to weed out any people who long to get rich quick. He may accept the one who knows when to restrain his desires (v. 4).

It is more probable, however, that verses 4 and 5 do not serve as a bridge between verse 3 and 6, that both passages (vv. 1–3 and vv. 6–8) speak of restraint at another's table, but for different reasons and under different circumstances. The reason I say this is that in one case the host is a ruler and in

---

1. Literally, "thinking" here means "counting up" what you are eating and how much is left.
2. Literally, "soul" (*nephesh*).

the other he is a stingy man. Two distinct scenarios seem to be in view.

Proverbs 26:4, 5

"Answer not a fool according to his folly."
"Answer a fool according to his folly"

Don't answer a stubborn fool according to his folly; otherwise, you will be like him. Answer a stubborn fool according to his folly; otherwise, he will be wise in his own eyes.

Well, which should you do? Answer or not? Both, of course. There is no contradiction here. Stylistically arranged so that one would remember these verses, the author placed them in juxtaposition to one another in a seeming contradictory – but, actually, contrasting – manner. Certainly, because they are striking, they not only attract attention and contemplation, but in addition, they are easily recalled.

But what do they mean? Well, the point of the verses turns on two of the meanings of the phrase "according to." In the first sentence, "according to" means "after the manner (or example) of," while in the second the phrase means "in an appropriate manner." Thus, the first sentence should be read "Don't answer a stubborn fool after the manner of his folly," and the second, "Answer the stubborn fool in a manner appropriate to his folly."

But what of the word "answer"? Does it imply a previous question? Not in this place. It more accurately has the meaning of "Respond to." So, the sentences would then read, "Don't respond to a stubborn fool after the manner of his folly," and, "Respond to a stubborn fool in a manner appropriate to his folly."

The second half of each sentence provides the clue from which we are able to make the distinction between the meanings of "according to." In the first, the warning is that if you respond in like fashion to the actions or words of the fool, you will be a fool like he is; so don't do it. That is to say, if he rages against you for some foolish reason, don't respond by raging in return. Rather, adopt a policy such as the one set forth in Proverbs 15:1, and give a soft answer.

The second sentence, however, makes it clear that you should not let the fool get away with his folly. If you do not respond by saying or doing something appropriate to (that is, something that will expose) his folly, he will think that he is pretty smart. Unless someone establishes for him a standard by which to judge his words and actions, he'll go on doing and saying such foolish things in the future.

So, while you must not act or speak in ways that are similar to those of the fool, in a proper manner you must respond to him so as to condemn his folly. Otherwise, he will wrongly evaluate what he did or said as fitting, appropriate or smart. He is no proper judge of his own wisdom; he is a fool. He, therefore, needs the help of another to set a biblical standard of speech and behavior before him. For more on judging others, see the entry in this volume on Matthew 7:1ff.

ECCLESIASTES 9:5

"The living know that they will die, but the dead don't know anything"

The living know that they will die, but the dead don't know anything. Nor do they have any more reward since their memory is forgotten.

Does this verse teach soul sleep, as some think? That, they aver, is clear from the fact that Solomon says the dead know nothing. The doctrine of soul sleep teaches that, upon death, human beings go out of conscious existence and are revived only at the resurrection. Others, who are annihilationists, believe that only the righteous dead will live forever, after being raised from the dead; the ungodly will be obliterated – i.e., no longer exist. Both views are wrong.

"Well, then, what does this passage teach?" you ask. Solomon is not talking about what the dead can or cannot do in eternity. His concern is the futility of the temporariness of "life under the sun." That is to say – as this phrase means – life lived for the here-and-now. It is, then, precisely not about the *state* of the dead after death that he writes, but about what death does to persons *with reference to life here on earth.*

His point, therefore, is that so far as this life is concerned, the dead are "out of it." They know nothing of what is happening in the world that they have left behind. They cannot make contact with it. If they have not settled their eternal destiny with God while alive, it is too late now to do so. The living at least have the knowledge that this is true – death is coming and they must prepare for it. It is too late to think about such things after death. So, a living dog is better than a dead lion – so far as what he can do on earth (v. 4). One's wealth, power or prestige in this world won't matter in the next. It will get him nothing.

It is interesting that, so far as the often asked question about whether or not the dead know what is happening on earth is concerned, the fifth verse seems to say, "No, they don't." And, so far as getting anything by way of reward or recognition posthumously is concerned, though men may reward them in one way or another, the dead cannot enjoy these rewards. And, indeed, these "rewards" (if they come at all) are not lasting, since the "memory" of those who have died soon fades away.

What happens on earth after one's death and what he can do about it, is vain so far as he is concerned. He is not here to reap the reward, he knows nothing about it and he cannot do anything to change circumstances. The emphasis in this verse, as throughout the book of Ecclesiastes, is to live not for this life (for what one can achieve "under the sun") but for the coming one. The latter, alone, is what lasts (for details, see my commentary on *Ecclesiastes, Life under the Sun/Son*).

ISAIAH 53:9

"And he made his grave with the wicked, and with the rich in his death"

And he made his grave with the wicked and with the rich in his death; because he had done no violence, neither was deceit found in his mouth.

Once again, we are confused by the King James translation. How is one to interpret the verse as it reads there? Surely, we know that there were two criminals crucified with the Lord and that a rich man, Joseph of Arimathea, donated his tomb for Jesus' burial place. Somehow, the verse seems to be getting at these facts, but it is hard to see how.

In a very informative article in the *Moody Monthly Magazine, September 1976,* Dr. Alan Macrae cleared up the confusion. He pointed out that this is "one of the least exact translations anywhere" in the King James Version. He then went on to say, "Its English words introduce ideas not in the original and omit ideas the Hebrew contains."

The verse, "properly translated," he goes on to say, "might better read: 'His grave was assigned with wicked men, but he was with a rich man in his death; because he had done no violence, neither was any deceit in his mouth.'" This translation is confirmed in essence by E.J. Young in his commentary on the verse.

Now the verse can be understood. Though others intended to bury Jesus together with the two thieves, and actually assigned Him to a grave with them (something that often took place when burying criminals), their plans were frustrated by Joseph, the rich man, who offered his own tomb. Thus, long beforehand, the prophecy set forth these unusual facts as they actually transpired.

The latter part of the verse gives the heavenly reason why this took place as it did. It was because Jesus did not deserve a criminal's burial since He had committed no crime.

MATTHEW 6:12, 14, 16

"but if you won't forgive people, neither will your Father forgive your trespasses."

> And forgive us our debts as we also have forgiven our debtors...Now if you forgive people their trespasses against you, so too your heavenly Father will forgive you; but if you won't forgive people, neither will your Father forgive your trespasses.

Many are troubled by these words. They say, "I thought all my sins, past, present and future were covered by the sacrificial death of Jesus Christ. What is this forgiveness after forgiveness?" The question is a good one, and is easy to answer once it is understood who is speaking to whom about what.

Who is speaking? God, the heavenly Father (Who was also addressed as such in the Lord's prayer). To whom? The heavenly Father is speaking to His children in Christ – all believers. About what? About trespasses and the forgiveness of the same

Now, it is clear that the words, "Neither will your Father forgive your trespasses," have nothing to do with salvation. The transaction referred to takes place among those who are His spiritual children. The issue of salvation is not in jeopardy. Christ has dealt with the matter once for all. Indeed, it was by His death on the cross for guilty sinners that those who trusted in Him as Savior were brought into the heavenly family (John 1:12). So, then, if salvation is not the issue before us, what is?

The Lord's prayer, and its footnote on forgiveness, have to do with *parental* forgiveness, not *judicial* forgiveness. The latter, as I just said, was settled for all time by the death of Christ for His people. The former, however, is an ongoing family matter. If a member of the family of God refuses to forgive others, the heavenly Father will refuse to forgive him until he does. In other words, He says, "Don't come to Me asking for forgiveness when you refuse to do the same for others." A similar idea clearly comes out in a specific situation. Peter says that if a Christian husband fails to treat his wife properly, his prayers will be hindered (I Peter 3:17).

If a child is doing something he knows is wrong and refuses to change his ways, yet expects to enjoy all the rights and privileges of an obedient child, he should not be surprised if his earthly father says, "No, you may not go out tonight using the car. There are matters you must settle with me first." He doesn't throw him out of the family, but he does *discipline* him as a member of it. That is the sort of thing about which Jesus is speaking here.

The easy answer to what at first seems difficult is that there are two kinds of forgiveness: judicial (from God as Judge) and parental (from God as Father). The word "Father" pervades the passage. It is plainly Fatherly forgiveness, then, that is in view.

MATTHEW 7:1, 2

"Judge not"

> Don't judge, or you will be judged; the same
> sort of judgment that you use in judging will be
> used to judge you; and the same sort of mea-
> sure that you use in measuring will be used to
> measure you.

How often has someone said, "Judge not!" when you were
evaluating something as good or bad, true or false, biblical or
unbiblical? The person triumphantly used the words of Matthew 7:1, expecting them to silence you once and for all,
didn't he? Well, did he use them rightly or not? Is that what
the passage means? Should you never make such evaluations?
It is important to understand Jesus' words about this matter.

Well, let's get one thing straight from the outset: these
words do *not* forbid judging. Jesus also told us to "Make a
right judgment" (John 7:24). And, note especially, no sooner
did He say "Don't judge, or you will be judged," than just five
verses later, He also commanded, "Don't give what is holy to
dogs; and don't throw your pearls before pigs" (v. 6). Obviously, to distinguish between those who are dogs or pigs and
those who are not requires judgment. And later on in the
chapter Jesus requires Christians to judge between true and
false prophets (vv. 15–23). So, as you can see by such examples, you *must* judge. Jesus requires it!. And at the last "*judgment*," (Matthew 25), it is clear that *distinguishing between
things* is the uppermost factor in judging. At that time, Jesus
will *divide* the sheep from the goats. But, notice, He will do so
on the basis of adequate data (which He mentions in vv. 35–
45). Similarly, He certainly does expect you to judge between
the true and the false, the biblical and the unbiblical, the good
and the bad.

So, are there contradictions in the Bible? Even more to the
point – does Jesus contradict Himself? Of course not. Both
here and in John 7, Jesus explains precisely what he means. In

Matthew 7:1, 2, Jesus qualifies the prohibition on judging by assuming you *will* judge and by telling you how to do so: with the measure (standard) you would want others to use in judging you! And, He warns, others will tend to judge you as you have judged them. In John 7 (it's easy to remember these two crucial passages because they both are found in a seventh chapter) Jesus also explained what He meant by a righteous judgment: it is one that is not "according to what appears on the surface."

So, when He says "Don't judge," He is not forbidding all judgment, but that judgment which is unrighteous. An unrighteous judgment is a superficial one – one that is made by considering only those surface factors that are immediately ascertained by a mere cursory look. He expects one to judge only after digging deeply into a situation, by gathering all the pertinent data. This is important, because, too often, we make fast opinions (judgments) of others or of their actions on the basis of too few facts. You would not like to be judged superficially, would you? No, of course you would not. Then, He says, don't judge others that way. That is Jesus' point in Matthew 7 and John 7.

Moreover, in a parallel passage (Luke 6:37) another word is added to the word *krino* ("judge") which is used here. It is *katadikadzo*, "to condemn." Poor judgment is that which condemns another apart from adequate facts. That is why God tells us to be careful about how we listen when we gather facts (cf. Proverbs 18:13, 15, 17).

Far from forbidding all judging, then, Matthew 7 is *instruction* about how to judge properly. In that regard, Jesus makes it clear that in order to judge another properly, he must first deal with the sin in his own life (He calls it a "log" in the eye; Matthew 7:5). That is, he must first judge himself. When one has removed his log, He says, he will be able to see to remove the "speck" in another's eye. This hyperbolic language is striking enough to make one think about his own faults and memorable enough to stick with him so that he will not forget it the next time he must judge another.

The hogs and the dogs mentioned in verse 6, along with the mention of "that which is holy" and "pearls," mean that a Christian is to be careful about picking specks out of the eyes of unbelievers – i.e., judging them. Instead, of course, what they need to hear is the gospel, not judgment, even by Christian standards. The dogs were the garbage collectors and could not distinguish holy meat (from the temple altar) from ordinary meat. To them it was all the same; they had no appreciation of the temple sacrifice that had occurred. Likewise, a pig would trample pearls under foot thinking at first it was food and disgusted when he discovered that it was not. Again, he would not appreciate the great value of what he was rejecting. Leave the log in the hog alone!

The idea, then, is that the unbeliever would fail to appreciate even the most well meant, righteous judgment of his behavior. Because it is not our task to reform an unbeliever, we engage in erroneous activity when we try to pick specks out of his eye; indeed, he may even become so agitated that, like the pig, he will turn and attack you. Instead, what he needs to hear from you is the gospel by which, if he believes, he may in time learn to appreciate criticism and judging rightly offered by a brother. Remember, it is hard enough to get a true Christian to accept helpful criticism!

MATTHEW 8:22

"Let the dead bury the dead"

And a different disciple said to Him, "Lord, let me first go and bury my father." But Jesus replied, "Follow Me, and leave the dead to bury their own dead."

Some have thought these words harsh and insensitive. But are they? Are they not the straightforward response of the Lord to one who was offering an excuse for failing to obey His command to follow Him? This is one of the places where the same word is used in two senses. The *spiritually* dead – those who had no understanding of why I am calling you – Jesus said, should bury the *physically* dead. There is obviously a play on these words.

But why was the command given? Jesus wanted followers who would be obedient and willing to do as He said. He would not call one unless it was proper for him to follow at that time. Jesus knew best. But here was a man who was hesitant; he was willing to divide his allegiance between the Lord and his family. It seems that he was either saying, "Let me remain at home until my father dies," or, "He has just died, and I must wait to follow until the ritual period for having touched the dead is over. Ceremonial defilement meant seven days of uncleanness (Numbers 19:11). That, too would be a delay. Either way, the Lord wanted those to follow Him who, like Matthew, rose up from his tax work and immediately did so (Matthew 9:9), and the fishermen who even left their nets to follow Him (Matthew 4:20, 22). There is a distinct contrast in the reactions of those men with the one who wanted to remain behind for a time.

MATTHEW 19:24

"It is easier for a camel to go through the eye of a needle..."

> Let Me assure you that it will be hard for a rich man to enter the kingdom from the heavens. Again I tell you, it is easier for a camel to go through the eye of a needle than for a rich man to enter into God's kingdom.

Because of the impossibility of a camel going through the eye of a needle, some have invented the idea that there must have been a gate that was so low to get through that it was called the eye of the needle. There is no historical evidence of the existence of such a gate. Besides, the notion that it refers to something that is barely possible rather than utterly impossible ruins the saying.

This hyperbolic saying of Jesus is akin to His comment that the religious leaders swallowed a camel and strained out a gnat (Matthew 23:24). That, again, refers to an impossibility. The idea behind both sayings is simply to refer to contrasting extremes. Riches, of course, do not really make it impossible to be saved (cf. I Timothy 6:17–19), though they may make it extremely difficult ("hard") as Jesus says.

The Talmud speaks of an elephant going through the eye of a needle when referring to something extremely difficult. Clearly, the idea was commonly abroad as a way of stating an impossibility.

Some literalists have great difficulty in understanding normal hyperbole, which people use all the time.[1] But even they, when confronted with Jesus' admonition to cut off the right hand or foot, leave their literalism behind! Hyperbole has the effect of shocking the listener into attention and thought, and of making a saying memorable. Once having heard about a camel going through the eye of a needle, you never forget it.

---

1. The phrase "all the time" is itself hyperbolic!

MATTHEW 25:31–46

"you did it to Me...
you didn't do it to Me."

> And the King will respond by saying to them:
> "Let Me assure you that insofar as you did it to
> one of the least of these, My brothers, you did it
> to me"...Then He will answer them, saying,
> "Let Me assure you that insofar as you didn't do
> it for one of the least of these, you didn't do it
> for Me."

"What? I thought that salvation was by grace, through faith – not by works." Has that question ever arisen in your mind as you read over the judgment scene in Matthew 25? Well, many believers have been troubled by it. Let's see how the passage in no way contradicts the consistent biblical teaching that salvation is not by works, "lest anyone should boast" (Ephesians 2:9).

First, notice that at the judgment who is a sheep and who is a goat is to be determined by what they *did* – their *works* (vv. 35–46). That is what confuses people who don't understand the biblical teaching about judgment. Many think that because judgment is by works, salvation must also be by works. But that is not true. All through the Bible a distinction between the two is carefully maintained. For instance, in Matthew 7, when discussing true and false prophets, Jesus says, "So it is from their fruits (works) that you will know them" (v. 20).

Well, then, how should we understand the judgment? The judgment is based on works, or "fruit." This is the great message of the book of James. During a powerful discussion of dead faith (faith that does not produce works[1]), James challenges those who say that they have faith but do not demonstrate it in their lives, and declares, "Show me your faith

---

1. False, not *saving* faith.

without works, and by my works I'll show you my faith" (James 2:18). What does he mean by that?

James' assertion is in complete accord with Jesus' words in Matthew 7 and 25. In all three places, that which *demonstrates* the presence of saving faith is works. It does not save but is the *evidence* of salvation. The true believer *will* do good works. He is a new creation and must do good works. He has been "created in Christ Jesus *for* good works" (Ephesians 2:10.

"Judgment" in the Bible carries the idea of *distinguishing* or *separating* between things that differ. On the Day of Judgment the King will *separate* the sheep from the goats. This point is emphasized in verse 32: "and all the nations will be assembled before Him, and He will separate them, one from another, as a shepherd separates the sheep from the goats." Some, erroneously, have thought that this means Jesus will separate *nations* from one another. That is not what He was speaking about. He was talking about individuals, just as He was when he spoke of discipling "all nations" in Matthew 28:18. Clearly, there He was talking about making disciples from among all nations. Here, too, the idea of people from all nations separated into two groups is in view.

One, therefore, is "saved" by grace, through faith alone. But saving faith is never alone; it always issues in good works (works that are pleasing to God). But when it comes to *determining* who is saved and who is not, that judgment is made on the basis of works. That is because, the only way to determine who is and who is not saved is by the outward behavior of the person who is judged. Though, of course, Jesus knows hearts, and would not need to separate the sheep from the goats on the basis of their outward words and actions, to demonstrate to all others present (surely including the angels) the judgment (separation) is made on the basis of works – the fruit of salvation.

Works, then, don't justify; they demonstrate one's justification. That is because *all* who have been regenerated and justified soon begin to put off the old patterns and put on the new ones. This process of sanctification alone, leads to works acceptable to God. People who have never been regenerated are still "in the flesh" and, as Paul said, "those who are in the flesh *cannot* please God" (Romans 8:8). Plainly, the "works" lauded by the Lord in Matthew 25 are pleasing to Him. They are, therefore, the fruit (works) of the Spirit, and not the works of the flesh.

MARK 3:28–30

"Whoever blasphemes against the Holy Spirit will never be forgiven."

> Let me assure you that all sorts of sinful acts and blasphemies spoken by the sons of men will be forgiven them, but whoever blasphemes against the Holy Spirit will never be forgiven, but rather will be held guilty for committing an eternal sin (this He said because some had claimed, "He has an unclean spirit").

It would be interesting to have a complete listing of all the explanations of what people think the unpardonable sin is. Some are certain that it is homosexuality, some taking the Lord's Name in vain, others that it is unbiblical divorce. And so it goes.

Sometimes counselees come to biblical counselors deeply concerned and fearful, wondering whether they might have committed this sin. Often, the counselor must say, "Let's talk first about the pardonable ones, then we will consider it!" After having dealt with those, rarely is the counselee concerned any longer. He recognizes that these pardonable sins were his true problem. Quickly, in this way, they come to see that a true Christian could never commit this sin.

But just what is the unpardonable sin, and why is it unpardonable? The context of our passage begins at Mark 3:22. Scribes from Jerusalem came down to where Jesus was, declaring, "He is possessed of Beelzebub" because "He casts out demons by the ruler of the demons." Jesus then told them a parable of the thief. He said that a man can steal a strong man's property only if he is stronger than he. By this, He made it clear that He was stronger than Satan, and as a result, was able to free people of the latter's demonic minions.

To the idea that Jesus cast out demons by the power of Beelzebub (another name for the devil), He responded by scoffing, pointing out that "a kingdom...divided against itself...can't stand" (v. 24). Two verses later, He reiterated this fact using the analogy of a house. Then, He showed them that it would be utterly foolish for Satan to empower Him to work against himself (v. 26). Having said these things, Jesus then uttered His fearful words about the unpardonable sin.

Is there any way of knowing what that sin is? Certainly; the answer to that question is embedded in the context of the incident. The unbelieving Scribes charged Jesus with casting out demons by the power of Satan, when it is clear that Jesus did so "by the Spirit of God," as we read in the parallel passage, Matthew 12: 28.

So, to say that Jesus cast out demons by the power of "the ruler of the demons" (Mark 3:22), is virtually to call the Holy Spirit the devil! That, Jesus says, is utterly unacceptable. They might accuse Him of being in league with the devil; that is one thing (Luke 12:10). But to speak that way against the Holy Spirit – No! The accusation meant that they called the Holy Spirit an "unclean spirit" (Mark 3:30, where the explanation is clearly set forth *as an explanation*). That charge is to impugn His essential nature. He is the *Holy* Spirit.

Those who think that the unpardonable sin takes place by committing some observable act err. It is, without doubt, something *spoken*, as we read in Mark 3:22, 30 ("they *said*, 'he is possessed by Beelzebub...he casts out demons by the ruler of demons'" and "some have *claimed*, 'he has an unclean spirit'"). That is, of course, what blasphemy is: hard words spoken to or about another. The hardest words that could be spoken against the Holy Spirit would be to call Him an *unclean* spirit.

Finally, a word about Beelzebub (or Beelzebul). The origin of the word is disputed. Clearly, it was a pejorative term. Some think that it means "the lord of manure," or "the lord of flies." The words of these Scribes showed their utter contempt for the Savior, and, as a result, this contempt reflected on the Holy Spirit, with Whom He had been anointed at His baptism.

LUKE 16:8

"The lord commended the dishonest steward because of his shrewd action."

The lord commended the dishonest steward because of his shrewd action. The sons of this age are more shrewd with people of their own kind than are the sons of light. So I tell you, make friends for yourselves with mammon of dishonesty, so that when it fails they will welcome you into the eternal dwellings.

The story to which this is the conclusion begins at the first verse of this chapter. The reader should familiarize himself with it. The problems with which we are concerned are:

1. how can the Lord Jesus "commend" a "dishonest steward?"

2. what is Mammon?

3. how does what Jesus says apply to Christians?

Consider the first matter. The Lord Jesus did not commend the steward for his dishonest acts. Obviously, that was far from His mind. Nor does He say that he dealt "wisely," as the King James Version translates. What he did was not wise. Rather, He commended his "shrewdness" or "prudence" (Greek, *phronimos*, not *sophos*) to those who were listening. So long as he had control of his master's estate, he used that power to provide for his future.

As Jesus did when he told the parable of the unjust judge, he used characters in this parable who illustrated something other than their sin. The injustice of both is merely there for the sake of the parable. But, in the case before us, it does also indicate how much more thought and effort the unbeliever puts into protecting himself from financial injury than a Christian does, even though the latter's efforts are intended to achieve *spiritual* aims. In pursuing the goals of the Kingdom of God, believers ought to be every bit as prudent, but in non-sinful ways. Indeed, their concern for their future ought to be

40

far greater, because it concerns what will take place in *eternal* dwellings.

The second issue concerns *mammon*. What is it? It is the accumulation of money that one may have. Jesus says to use that money shrewdly *now*. Use it to bless others so long as you are here in this world. Do it so that you may have many believers gratefully welcome you into your eternal home when you die and must leave all your accumulation of money behind.[1] In other words, make your money here reap eternal dividends.

The "mammon of dishonesty" means the mammon that the shrewd steward *used* dishonestly. Jesus isn't saying that we must use money dishonestly, or that all accumulation of money is dishonest, or that every accumulation that one has was obtained dishonestly. He is saying the very opposite. Money – which in the steward's case was used dishonestly to gain friends for his earthly welfare – ought to be used honestly to make *eternal* friendships. A Christian cannot serve God and mammon. He must use it for the welfare of others and thus obtain eternal benefit for them and for himself.

The problem, in answer to the third question, is that unbelievers deal more shrewdly or prudently with other unbelievers than Christians do with other Christians (v. 8[b]). That is something to contemplate. Indeed, it is an indictment against the foolishness of believers who think only of using their wealth for earthly ends. The real question is, "How may you use the money you have accumulated to 'make friends' who someday will greet you in your eternal home?" Most Christians haven't even given thought to this matter – let alone prudently calculated how they may make such friends. The passage ought to be considered by every Christian.

---

1. Some of those may be persons who have come to Christ through your giving to the preaching of the gospel.

JOHN 1:51

"...angels of God ascending and descending upon the Son of Man."

> He said to him, "Let Me tell you all something. You are going to see the sky open and God's angels ascending and descending before the Son of Man."

What in the world does this mean? Is Jesus Himself a ladder or stairway like that which Jacob saw, upon which angels moved to and from heaven (Genesis 28:12, 13)? What kind of sense would there be to that?

In the dream that Jacob had, "the Lord stood above it" (v. 13). Here, the Lord, Jesus Christ, was *below* the ladder. He has come as "Immanuel," God *with* us. That is the significant factor in the word of the Lord Jesus. That same Lord, Whose transcendence was clear in Jacob's vision, has now also demonstrated His immanence. He has become one of us, walking, talking with us, and living our life here below the ladder.

Yet there is still contact with heaven. The Father and the Son are in communication with One Another by means of angelic messengers who constantly move up and down the symbolic ladder.

But what of the word "upon"? The verse seems to say that Jesus is the ladder of communication between man and God. That, of course, is true. But that is not what is taught here. The Greek word, translated "upon" (*epi*) of course may have that meaning. But it also may be translated other ways as well. In situations where motion is in view (as here) it may mean "toward, near, to, before." Any of these words would more appropriately describe the scene. The angels were ascending and descending to and from the Lord Jesus Christ, or "before" Him.

The interesting thing is the order in which the angels were moving on the ladder. They are first said to be ascending, then descending. That could mean at least two things:

that Jesus was continually sending messages to His Father about His work on earth, and/or that the authority of God was given to and was being exercised by Him on earth. Either way, the contact of Christ with heaven, from which He received His authority and power as the God-*man*, is in view. But that He identified with us in our humanity is seen by His reference to Himself as "the Son of Man."

JOHN 14:26

"He is the One
Who will teach you everything"

But the Counselor, the Holy Spirit that the
Father will send in My name, He is the One
Who will teach you everything and remind you
of everything that I told you.

"If so," you ask, "how come there are so many things I
don't know? And how come there are so many Christians
who differ about so many things? Has God failed to keep this
promise?"

Of course not. The problem is that in reading passages,
many have the harmful tendency of failing to ask, "To whom
is this passage speaking?" This verse does not contain a general promise that is given to every believer. It is a promise
that the Lord made to His disciples about what would happen
to them when they became apostles who would preach and
write His Word under inspiration. We know this because the
promise appears in a section of Scripture in which Jesus had
drawn His disciples away from others in order to institute His
Supper, and instruct them about what would happen after His
death and resurrection. That the passage pertained to them
alone is perfectly clear from the verse itself. Jesus promised
that the Spirit would remind them (as well as teach them) of
all the things He had told them before. Thus, in fulfillment of
the promise, they were enabled by the Spirit to write the Gospel accounts.

It is, then, a promise that the Holy Spirit would inspire
them to proclaim by word and by pen the truths He had
taught them directly and those that He would tell them later
through inspiration. It is not a promise for every believer of
every age.

There is, however, a secondary element in the promise that
does pertain to believers of every age since. Because the
promise was fulfilled in the production of the New Testament,

we benefit from those twenty-seven books just as if the promise were made to us. But all notions of the Spirit still teaching *us* new truth that goes beyond the Scriptures is forbidden (cf. II John 8, 9). Think about it: if the apostles were taught "everything" that is needed, it is obvious that there is nothing more yet to come. The verse gives the lie to all who claim revelation today.

JOHN 16:7–11

"He will convict the world about sin, about righteousness and about judgment."

> If I don't go away, the Counselor certainly won't come to you; but if I go, I will send Him to you. When he comes, He will convict the world about sin, about righteousness and about judgment: about sin – because they don't believe in Me, about righteousness – because I am going to the Father and you won't see me any more, and about judgment – because this world's ruler has been judged.

What does this mean? That's the question. The context helps us to know. The Lord spoke about how the disciples would be "put out of the synagog" and how people would even be delighted to see them put to death (John 16:2). Hard times would lie ahead. Jesus said that He didn't tell them about the persecution earlier because He was with them to care for them. But now that He was leaving, they needed to know. The negative focus that had been on Him would now shift to them. Yet, they would not be alone to face it because He would send the Holy Spirit (vv. 4–7).

The Spirit would not be inactive when He came. He would supply them with all of the help they needed to face and defeat their persecutors. Indeed, He would turn the tables on them. They would haul the disciples up before their courts, but in those days, the Holy Spirit would be their Counselor-at-law and convict their enemies of their crimes (vv. 7, 8).

The conviction would be about sin, righteousness and judgment. What did that mean? He delineates what he meant about each. "About sin – because they don't believe in Me." That means that the Spirit will prove that those who refused to trust Him as Savior are unforgiven, still in their sins. "About righteousness – because I am going to My Father and you won't see Me any more." He meant that the Holy Spirit would prove His case that the words and the works of Christ were righteous. How? By the fact of His going to the Father (the resurrection and the ascension); that would be enough to prove the case. The empty tomb still is unexplained by the world. And, finally, "about judgment – because this world's ruler has been judged." That had in view the fact that Satan was being defeated by Jesus Who "bound the strong man," and took captive many of his subjects as He wrested the dominion from him (Colossians 2:13–15). That, of course, meant that those who opposed the disciples were staking their stand with a defeated foe.

JOHN 17:21

"That they all may be one"

...that all may be one just as You, Father, are
with Me and I with You; that they too may be
with Us, so that the world may believe that You
sent Me.

Unity! Everyone agrees that is what Jesus was talking
about in John 17 in His prayer for the disciples and those who
would believe through their ministries. But, sadly, the liberals
who have touted the passage as their warrant for organizational, ecumenical unity (apart from doctrinal unity) have
promoted their views so successfully that conservative, Bible
believing Christians also have been duped into thinking that
organizational unity is mandated here. Usually, conservatives
have modified the supposed mandate to include forms of doctrinal agreement, but, like the liberals, they still maintain the
mistaken idea that Jesus prayed for organizational unity. If
that is the true intent of Jesus' words, then clearly, He was a
false prophet!

"Jesus a false prophet?" you ask. Yes, exactly that – if
organizational unity is what He had in view. Read the latter
half of the verse. The unity of which He spoke had a particular goal in sight: "so that the world may believe that You sent
Me." In the history of the Church there has been more organizational division than there has been unity. There has been
a great deal of doctrinal disagreement as well. If the world was
to believe on the basis that Christianity is one organization-
ally (or even doctrinally), then the world has seen precious
little unity of the sort the would lead to faith.

No! That is not what Jesus was talking about. Note, in this
verse, there is no horizontal unity mentioned. The unity is
strictly vertical. And it has nothing to do with organization at
all. Jesus was concerned that the disciples and other believers
be one with Himself, just as (in just the way that) He is one
with the Father. That is the concern all through the prayer (cf.

also vv. 11, 23, 24). Jesus would hardly have been speaking of *organizational* unity with the Father!

Christ's theme in the prayer is that the Father would "guard" His disciples (v. 12) so that none of them would be lost, as Judas was. He "kept" or "guarded" them while He was with them. Now that He was leaving, He wanted them to continue to be protected. He wanted them to be "kept" from the wiles of the evil one (v. 15). So, he prayed for their sanctification (vv. 16, 17); that is, that the Father would "set them apart"[1] to Himself.

So what is the unity that would lead unbelievers to believe? It is unity with Himself – the fact that true believers would be in as secure a unity with Himself as He was with the Father. That they would all be one with Him. That He would lose none whom the Father set apart for Himself. It is the security that would come through unity of the believer with Christ that is in view.

How did that manifest itself? And did unbelievers become believers as a result? Yes, they did. One of the principal ways in which the early church gained converts (and how it does so around the world today where persecution abounds) was that Christians maintained their faith when burned at the stake, thrown to lions, or tortured on the rack. In answer to His Son's prayer, the Father "kept" them in such hours. Their endurance, and firm adherence to Christ, impressed others and became a witness that brought many to faith.

Let us be thankful that Jesus Christ did not pray for some failed organizational unity of believers with one another, but that He was asking the Father to keep them – you – in unity with the Trinity itself! Your eternal security depends not on your own personal efforts but, fundamentally, upon the unfailing prayer of the Lord Jesus Christ.

---

1. This is the meaning of the word "sanctify."

JOHN 20:21–23

"Receive the Holy Spirit"

> So Jesus said to them again, "Peace to you. As
> the Father sent Me, so also do I send you,"
> When He had said this, He breathed on them
> and said to them, "Receive the Holy Spirit. If
> you forgive anybody's sins, they are forgiven; if
> you retain them, they are retained."

Ask ten Christians, "When was the New Testament
Church organized?" and more likely than not all ten will tell
you "On the Day of Pentecost." But is that so? Jesus said to
the apostles "you will receive power (*dunamis*) when the
Holy Spirit has come upon you, and you will be My witnesses
in Jerusalem, in the rest of Judea, and to the ends of the earth"
(Acts 1:8). Pentecost was a commission and empowerment of
a body to preach the Gospel in all the world; there is nothing
on that occasion that would indicate that the Church was
being organized. Organization would involve authority
(*exousia*) rather than power (*dunamis*).

Indeed, Jesus had already given them post-resurrection
instructions about the organization and conduct of His "kingdom."[1] This took place over a forty day period (Acts 1:2, 3). It
seems clear, then, that prior to that time He had organized the
entity about which Jesus was now instructing the apostles.
When did that organization take place?

On the first day of the week, Jesus appeared to the disciples
who were meeting in a room with the door shut (John 20:19).
He greeted them with the words "Peace be to you." Then,
after showing them the marks in His hands and side, He said
to them again, "Peace to you. As the Father sent Me, so also I
do I send you." Then, "when He had said this, He breathed on
them and said to them, 'Receive the Holy Spirit. If you forgive anybody's sins, they are forgiven; if you retain them,

---

1. Another word for the New Testament church.

they are retained'" (vv. 21–23). What are we to make of this event?

Clearly, it indicates that the apostles had received the Holy Spirit prior to Pentecost, an event that reached beyond their number to all those who had gathered together on that occasion. Pentecost was a public announcement to the world (or, at least to the Jews,) that the Church was now moving forward on its mission. But there is nothing to indicate that this was a time of organization or receiving of authority to do the work of Christ. The Church on that occasion did not take shape, it was already in existence and was now commencing the task outlined by Christ in Acts 1:8.

In contrast, the encounter that took place in the closed room, recorded in John 20, *was* an authority-giving event. Jesus' breathing on the apostles, thus symbolizing His impartation of the Holy Spirit, and His accompanying words, granted them the *authority* to forgive and retain sins. That, of course, is the mission of the Church: to preach the good news by which men's sins might be forgiven. The words that the apostles preached proclaimed both the retention and the forgiveness of sins. Those who believed were forgiven, and became members of the visible Church through baptism; those who did not, were left outside the Church. That was what the missionary preaching of the apostles was all about.

The Church of Jesus Christ, then, was organized in the closed room. It was an event that had to do with the Church alone; others were not present. Only its chief representatives and organizers were present. The door, closed "for fear of the Jews," also shut out others from the organizational meeting at which Jesus handed over His mission to the apostles and those who would follow in their stead. Note, carefully, His word, "As the Father sent Me, so also do I send you." Here was the commission of the Church to take up the work that Jesus Christ has done while on earth. He was now leaving the scene, and was handing over the work to them. Here was the beginning of what He had predicted earlier in the upper room when He said, "whoever believes in Me will himself do the works that I am doing; indeed, he will do greater works than these because I am going to the Father" (John 14:12). He had told them that His works would be limited because He was leaving them. They, in turn, would take up where He had left off, and because He was leaving, they would do more works ("greater" in number) that He. On that occasion, He also spoke freely about the coming Holy Spirit, Who would be their Counselor instead of Him. The Spirit would remind and teach them all that they needed to know to found the Church (John 14:26). It seems obvious that the reception of the Spirit spoken of in this upper room discourse (John 14) was not principally His coming at Pentecost, but the coming in the room with the closed door. It was a coming to the apostles as the founders (organizers) of the Church.

That founding function was limited to the apostles; no others were a part of it. Paul wrote: "So then, you are no longer strangers and aliens, but rather you are citizens together with the saints and members of God's household, built on the foundation of the apostles and prophets, with Christ Jesus Himself as the chief Cornerstone" (Ephesians 2:19, 20). And, he goes on to say, "the whole building [the church] being fitted together grows into a holy temple in the Lord. In Him, you are being built together into a place for God to dwell by His Spirit" (Ephesians 2:21, 22).

In other words, the Holy Spirit, given to the apostles on the occasion we are studying, so worked in and through the apostolic leadership that they were able to found and begin the building of Christ's Church, which is pictured as a temple in which God would dwell. Exactly as Jesus predicted, the Spirit enabled them to teach what the Church needed to know – that which was "revealed to His holy apostles and prophets by the Spirit" (Ephesians 3:5). Once more, it was to a particular gift of the Spirit to the "founders" of the Church, enabling them to know what to do to take up the work Jesus bequeathed to them, that Paul referred. In other words, many passages that have to do with the Spirit in relation to the apostles do not have reference to Pentecost, but to the gift of the Spirit that took place at the founding of the Church. These, we have seen, refer to the gift of the Spirit to the apostles at its founding which is recorded in John 20:19–23.

In Acts 1:14 and following, there is recorded for us the first act of the Church, in which a successor to Judas was appointed. This was an act of the Church, *as Church*. In doing so, Peter said, "It is written in the Book of Psalms, '…Let a different person take his office of oversight'" (Acts 1:20). The word translated "office of oversight" is "episcopate" (from *episcopos*, *"overseer"*). The episcopos was the primary *office* (or "work") of the elder. The election of this successor to Judas was an official act of the *Church*. Clearly, the body thought of the Church as in existence, with members, who had the right to elect this successor.[1]

Peter's prayer shows that they had already considered themselves a body with a mission, the apostles being at its head. He prayed, "Lord, Heart-Knower of all men, show which one of these two You have chosen to *take the place in this ministry and apostleship* from which Judas fell away to go to his own place" (Acts 1:24, 25). And, Matthias, being elected, "was counted along with the eleven apostles" (v. 26). This, again, seems to be an official *reckoning*. If he was "counted" such, the question is, by whom? The answer is: by the Church which elected him.

---

1. There is some question about whether the Church acted precipitously or not. Could the apostle Paul have been God's successor to Judas? But, apart from this fact, there is no doubt that the apostles and their disciples already considered themselves an organized body, with the right to act as such.

JOHN 21:17

"He said to him the third time, 'Do you care for Me?'"

> He said to him a third time, "Simon, son of John, do you care for Me?" Peter was deeply hurt that He said to him the third time, "Do you care for Me?" He said to Him, "Lord, You know everything, You know that I care for You!" Jesus said to him "Feed my sheep."

Peter had denied Jesus three time, just as Jesus had prophesied. When he realized his perfidy he wept. Thinking that he was through as a disciple, he went back to fishing. But after His resurrection, Jesus made a point to restore Peter by the seaside. The conditions reminded Peter of his faithlessness. There was a charcoal fire, just like the one around which Peter denied Him before the servant girl. There were three questions – one for each denial. Surely, Peter was delighted to see his Lord (he jumped into the sea to swim to him as soon as he realized it was Jesus; v. 7). But he was troubled over the reminders of his denials.

But what was it that most troubled him? What was it that so "deeply hurt?" Many think that it was because Jesus asked Him not once, not twice, but three times if he loved him. Yet, that is not the real point of the verse. The King James obscures the facts by it failure to distinguish two verbs that are used.

Jesus asked, "Simon, son of John, do you love Me more than these?" (v. 15). The comparison between him and the other disciples ("these") was made because of Peter's proud boast in Mark 14:29 where he indicated that if all the rest forsook Christ, he would not. But the important question was did Peter love Christ? Jesus in asking used the stronger word for love (*agapao*), but Peter responded with the weaker work "to care for" (*phileo*). The second time that Jesus asked, once again He used the strong word and Peter responded with the weaker one. Why is it that Peter did so? Probably, because he remembered his denials and was hesitant to claim rich, deep, abiding love. So, he used the lesser word.

Then, Jesus Himself used the lesser word, virtually asking "Peter, do you even *care* for Me?" Peter was deeply grieved at this change of words and cried out in agonized faith that the Lord knew all things and, therefore, He surely knew that he did care for Him. It was the change of verbs, then, that brought about the deep pangs of hurt into Peter's soul, not the number of times Jesus asked the question.

But, having brought Peter through the depths of repentance, Jesus restored him three times to his ministry. And Peter, a new man, went on to courageously live and die for Him (as Jesus predicted in v. 18). The three restorations corresponded to the three denials. Jesus was gracious to *completely* restore His erring disciple. When it was over, there was no doubt of the fact.

Acts 9:7; 22:9

"Hearing a voice..."
"...they heard not the voice"

> The men who were traveling with him stood speechless, hearing the sound of a voice, but seeing nobody...Now those who were traveling with me saw the light as well, but they didn't understand what the voice that spoke to me said.

There is no doubt that the inaccurately translated words of the King James Version unnecessarily create a contradiction and, thereby have caused confusion. The verse in Acts 9:7, in the original, reads "heard *of* a voice" meaning that they heard the *sound* of the voice. That does not indicate that they understood what they heard at all.

On the other hand, the words in Acts 22:9 plainly say that they didn't understand the voice. The cases of the nouns make the difference. So, there is no contradiction between the two accounts after all. Those who swear by the King James Version should realize that there are faults in this translation just as there are in others. Even the New King James Version fails to make the correction. It should be a lesson to those who will look at no other version that all have their weaknesses and strengths. And exclusive King James devotees should remember that Jesus and the apostles themselves used *two* versions – the Hebrew and the Greek Septuagint, the latter of which was quoted more often than the former!

ACTS 17:22

"Men of Athens, everything I see shows how very religious you are."

> Then Paul stood up in the midst of the council of the Areopagus and said, "Men of Athens, everything I see shows me how very religious you are."

Was Paul commending these pagan Greeks? Certainly not! Well, then, was he buttering them up? To ask the question is to answer it. If neither of these explanations is apropos, then what did he mean by the words quoted above?

Understand the circumstances. Paul was alone in Athens, but he was no tourist. He did not admire the temples, the altars and the statues depicting pagan gods and goddesses. In verse 16 we read, "he was enraged within as he looked at the city filled with images." Beauty of sculpture and architecture was far from his concerns. Idolatry greatly offended him. Here was the supposed intellectual center of the world filled with idols! It was said that it was easier to find an image in Athens than a man. There were more statues in Athens than in all other Greek cities combined. That is what struck Paul! And so you may rest assured that this statement was irony at its best.

But that isn't all. It must be remembered that this preliminary hearing was being conducted to find out whether it would be necessary to bring Paul to trial. The Areopagus council was the body that licensed religion and determined whether or not one might propagate a new religion in the city. It was this same body that, years before, had condemned Socrates to death on two charges: corrupting the youth and setting forth new gods. Here was Paul being brought before them on a charge similar to one of those: "He seems to be promoting some foreign gods" (v. 18). Surely, Paul – trained in Greek, Latin and Hebrew literature – would know of Socrates' fate.

So, he begins his discourse by observing how religious

they were. It was not a compliment but an observation, as he goes on to note in the next verse. The statement was an introduction to the point he wanted to make. He went on to say:

> For example, as I was passing along, looking at your objects of worship, I even found an altar with this description: TO AN UNKNOWN GOD. So then, what you worship in ignorance is that which I am announcing to you!

At once he had deflected any charge of setting forth a new religion and had given himself an entrée into what he wanted to say.

Of course, he did not really believe that they were worshipping the true God under that altar. Rather, what he had in mind was to legitimize what he was saying before the council so that they could not charge him with "promoting some foreign (unlicensed) gods." Surely, those sharp philosophers and statesmen who were listening must have thought, "Pretty clever! He got us with that one!" Paul then went on to condemn every teaching of Epicureanism and Stoicism as he set forth the contrary truths of the gospel.

There are those who think that Paul made a mistake here, because he had so little effect on the crowd. First, remember, all his speeches were inspired.[1] So, he couldn't have spoken wrongly. And, look at the results closely: "some scoffed, but others said, 'We want to hear you speak about this again.'"...But some men joined him and believed, among whom were Dionysius the Areopagite and a women named Damaris, and others with them" (vv. 32, 34).

If you gave one talk at Harvard and had as converts a trustee and a famous person, along with others, you'd consider it a pretty good day's work, wouldn't you? To convert a member of the council, a well-known woman, and others, was a very good result in this intellectual center of the world! And there were others who wanted to hear him again!

---

1. See my book, *Preaching According to the Holy Spirit,* for proof of this statement.

ROMANS 15:13

"An abundance of hope by the power of the Holy Spirit"

Now may the God of hope fill you with every sort of joy and peace in believing, so that you may have an abundance of hope by the power of the Holy Spirit.

This passage has led some to conclude that, if they need hope, what they must do is ask God for it and by the power of the Holy Spirit hope will well up within them. When it didn't happen that way, they became perplexed, a fact that added to their discouragement and the shattering of whatever hope they had before. What is the solution to the problem? Does God infuse hope into us by His Spirit or doesn't He?

Well, the passage did not mislead. It was the failure of the interpreter that misled. God certainly *does* give His children hope – even an abundance of hope, as the verse says. Moreover, joy and peace come along with it! But these things do not come automatically, merely for the asking. How, then, does the Holy Spirit release His power in order to give us hope?

The answer is found in the context (as, indeed, the answers to many questions are). In verse 4 of the same chapter of Romans, Paul had already written about the matter, telling us how hope may be obtained. Here is what he said

> Whatever was written before was written for our instruction, that by the endurance and the encouragement that the Scriptures give us we may have hope

Now, it is clear from these words Paul didn't think that hope came merely for the asking. There are, as he makes very clear, means necessary for obtaining hope. Hope, he says, comes from the Scriptures. The Scriptures of the Old and the New Testaments (here he refers to the Old Testament) were written for those who would live at a later time. They were not only for the contemporaries of the Scripture writers. They belong to all of God's people for all time.

Here, he affirms that, *through the Scriptures,* believers are able to endure hardship and find the encouragement that leads to hope. Far from being automatic, the release of the power of the Holy Spirit comes through the study, application, and implementation of biblical truth. After all, the Bible is peculiarly *His* book. He inspired its writing, and it is through this instrument of His that He works in power to help His people.

Those, then, who seek hope in whatever seemingly hopeless situation they find themselves will not receive it as the result of strong desire, agonizing prayer or anything of the like. It is not up to us to suggest to God how He should impart His hope when He has already gone on record telling us how we may obtain it. And note: all hope comes from Him – He is the "God of hope." Study of the promises found in the Bible brings hope. The application of biblical commands when facing dire need brings hope. The implementation of biblical ways and means while going through trials brings hope. In short, hope comes through the Scriptures.

So, in the seemingly hopeless circumstances of life, rather than allow these to drive you farther away from God and His Word, use them to help you renew your interest in what He has said about them. Turn to His Word – and find help and hope.

I CORINTHIANS 7:12

"To the rest I, not the Lord, say..."

To the rest I (not the Lord) say: if any brother has an unbelieving wife and she agrees to live with him, he must not divorce her. And a woman who has an unbelieving husband who agrees to live with her, she must not divorce him.

Are there passages in the Bible that are uninspired? Isn't that what Paul was saying? Certainly not. Then, what do the words "not the Lord" mean?

What Paul is saying is that the "Lord" (Jesus) spoke about marriage and divorce as it pertained to two believers, but He did not have occasion to consider and give His Word on the matter of a believer married to an unbeliever.

Missionary activity outside the covenant community often led to one person in a marriage being converted, while the other remained unconverted. That meant that Paul was confronting a new situation – one about which the Lord did not speak when He was on earth. Now Paul was giving equally-inspired revelation about this new situation.

I CORINTHIANS 9:9

"It isn't about oxen
that God is concerned, is it?"

It is written in Moses' law, "Don't muzzle an ox
when it is threshing." It isn't about oxen that
God is concerned, is it?

In I Corinthians 9, Paul is talking about remuneration in
the ministry. His point is that those who minister should be
supported from their work just as a soldier, a farmer or a
shepherd is (v. 7). The work itself should provide the necessi-
ties for his life. In support of this viewpoint – which he says is
not merely a human one but, rather, goes back to the law of
Moses – he cites the passage "Don't muzzle an ox when it is
threshing" (Deuteronomy 25:4). Then, he asks the rhetorical
question (from which he expects the negative response, "of
course not") "It isn't about oxen that God is concerned, is it?"
He even goes on to say, "Isn't he really speaking about us?"
(I Corinthians 9:10).

Now, there are those who seem puzzled about this citation,
and Paul's ensuing comment. They ask, "It sure seems to me
that Moses *was* concerned about oxen. How does Paul infer
that he wasn't?" That is the problem.

Well, first of all, let's be sure we understand the implication of the words in question. Paul is saying that just as an ox
was allowed to eat some of the grain that he was threshing,
and that it was from the very work that he was doing that he
earned his keep, so too ministers of the Word should "reap
material benefits" from those to whom they minister
(I Corinthians 9:11). He says that Moses was talking about
paying ministers.

Well, the confusion comes from a poor understanding of
the way in which the New Testament writers interpreted the
Old Testament. Paul certainly wasn't denying oxen access to
the grain that they were threshing. Far from it! Nor was he
saying that the quotation from Deuteronomy did not really

refer to oxen. What he was affirming was that Moses had written under one application, that of oxen, a much larger *principle* that refers to human beings as well. Indeed, it refers to soldiers, to farmers, to shepherds, to plowmen, to threshers – and to preachers. That is to say, the principle refers to human beings primarily. God's concern for human beings is much greater than His concern for oxen; that is the point.

How much should a preacher be paid? That question frequently arises among elders, deacons and members of congregations. Too often, the question is answered arbitrarily. However, there is a clear standard for payment set forth in Galatians 6:6: "Now let him who is instructed in the Word share everything good that he has with the one who instructs him." This important verse is often bypassed in discussions of payment. But it should not be.

The standard that Paul holds before churches is that the church members should provide a salary for the minister that accords with the way in which the members live. "*Everything* good" that they have, he too should have. His standard of living should be consonant with theirs. How they may arrive at the amount may, then, possibly be determined by taking an average of the salaries of the members of the congregation.

At any rate, pastors should be paid from the work that they do (they should not have to derive their salaries from some other source) and they should be paid a salary that allows them to live on the same basis as members of their congregations.

I CORINTHIANS 9:27

"Lest...when I have preached to others, I myself should be a castaway."

Rather, I beat down my body and make it a slave so that I who have preached to others may not myself become disqualified.

Can a true believer, not to speak of a preacher like the apostle Paul, ever lose his salvation? Some have taken these words to mean just that. Paul is using strong language in this verse to show how he makes vigorous efforts to not allow his body to control him.[1] Rather, he "beats it down" to bring it under control for his service to the Lord.

But he is not concerned about losing his salvation; his concern is about that service to the Lord. He did not want to be rejected – struck off the list of contestants – so that he was no longer useful to his Lord.

He had been using athletic metaphors to describe his ministry. In the previous verse he said, "I don't run like somebody without a goal; I don't box like somebody who is beating the air (I Corinthians 9:26). Here, in verse 27, he continues the athletic imagery saying that he didn't want to be disqualified from a lack of self-control (v. 25). Understanding the imagery clears up the seeming difficulty.

---

1. Literally, he says that he beats it black and blue (or gives it a black eye).

I CORINTHIANS 13:8–13

"When that which is complete comes, that which is partial will be set aside."

Love never fails. If there are prophecies, they will be set aside; if there are languages, they will cease; if there is knowledge, it will be set aside. We know in part and we prophesy in part, but when that which is complete comes, that which is partial will be set aside. When I was a child I spoke like a child, thought like a child, I reasoned like a child; but now that I have become a man I have set aside childish ways. Now we see dimly as if looking in a bronze mirror, then face to face; now I know partially, but then I shall know fully just as I am known. Now these three things continue: faith, hope, love; and the greatest of these is love.

Here is a very important passage that has been wrongly understood because of the popularity of certain hymns that perpetuate the misunderstanding. For instance, we sing, "I shall see Him face to face," referring the passage to the coming of Jesus Christ. While what the hymn says is certainly true – we shall see Jesus face to face someday – the passage before us does not teach anything at all about the second coming or about seeing Him at death. Indeed, there is nothing about seeing Jesus here either. Well, then what does I Corinthians 13:8–13 teach?

To understand Paul's words you must understand the context as well. In chapters 12 and 14 he is discussing the matter of spiritual gifts, and is concerned to correct certain abuses that have to do with their use. He is interested in keeping people from misusing these gifts and, especially, from concentrating on the more spectacular ones, such as the gift of tongues, or, as the Greek word means, "languages." (Some Christians in the apostolic age were granted the ability to speak in foreign languages without having first studied them.) He wants believers to say and do those thing that will edify one another when they come together in meetings of the church. It is in the context of these two chapters that these verses appear. Chapter thirteen is intended to lay a basis for the correction of the misuses of gifts which were prevalent in the period from 30–70AD, as Joel had prophesied (see Joel 2, Acts 2).[1]

The words "face to face" and the words "then I shall know fully, just as I am fully known," are the ones that cause the difficulty. In discussing the Corinthians' unloving use of the gifts, which were imparted through Paul, as an apostle (I Corinthians 1:4–7), Paul says that these gifts were not for one's personal benefit, but for the benefit of all. He deplored their selfish use, because it was opposed to the love that he describes in chapter 13. The gift of tongues was a sign for unbelievers, so that the message could go quickly into all the world (I Corinthians 14:22), and was not to be used in church meeting without interpretation. Prophecy, in the church context, he says, is more useful than tongues because it edifies.

It seems that direct revelation was given in both tongues-speaking and prophecy. If a person could speak for God in a language he did not know, and could not interpret, there was something automatic rather than thoughtful about it. Why did these churches receive revelation from God apart from the Scriptures when we do not? The answer is found in our passage.

Here are some facts:

1. Paul makes it clear that the gifts of prophecy, tongues and special knowledge were but temporary (v. 8): he says that they will be "set aside" and will "cease."

2. Prophecies, will be "set aside." By whom? Presumably by the One Who gave them through the apostles – God. The word translated "set aside" is *katargeo*, which means "to set aside by annulling or abolishing." The language makes it

---

1. For more details on this see my book, *Signs and Wonders in the Last Days*.

plain that an outside force would act upon the prophet. Prophecies do not "annul" themselves!

3. The gift of speaking in foreign languages would "cease." The reason that the word *pauo* ("cease") was used rather than *katargeo* may be because it would peter out, rather than be brought to an abrupt ending. However, the change in verbs may be merely stylistic (the chapter is poetic).

4. The gift of knowledge – of direct, revelatory knowledge of facts, truth of various sorts – would be "set aside"; that is, would also be brought to an end by an outside force.

5. Now, in contrast to those three gifts, Paul assures us that faith, hope and love would continue. The word *meno* means "to remain, stay in place, continue."

Why the contrast? Paul makes it clear that those gifts that would be done away with were "partial" (v. 9). He says that we know in part and prophecy in part. That was the problem with these gifts – they were partial. This partial revelation will, he goes on to say, be replaced by a complete one.

To make this point, he provides two illustrations (vv. 11, 12). They both show how the lesser is replaced by the greater. Adult ways replace childish ones, and seeing face to face replaces looking in a mirror. There is nothing about heaven, eternal life, or the second coming in the passage. It would all take place here on earth when the partial revelatory gifts were replaced by that which is "complete."

How do we know that Paul is not speaking about the cessation of these gifts at Christ's coming? Verse 13 provides the answer to that question. In it Paul says that all three qualities – faith, hope, love – remain when the special gifts will be done away with. But, note, one of those remaining qualities is "hope" – the expectation of things to come. Why would hope remain at Christ's coming? It would be placed by the reality for which the believer hopes. In Paul's discussion of this very point in Romans 8:20–25, he makes it explicit that once the reality appears there is no longer reason to hope. He says, "But when you see what you hope for, that isn't hope. Who hopes for what he sees?" (v. 24).

It is certain, therefore, that I Corinthians 13 has a time in view when the revelatory gifts will be done away with, that is during this present life. A complete revelation, which would replace the partial ones, Paul says, would come. When it did, these partial means would no longer be needed. That revelation, of course, was the fully completed New Testament.

EPHESIANS 4:23

"Being renewed in the spirit of your mind"

You were taught regarding your previous habit patterns to put off the old person that you were, who is corrupted by deceitful desires, being rejuvenated in the attitude of your mind, and to put on the new person that you are, who is created in God's likeness with righteousness and holiness that comes from the truth.

The phrase "the spirit of your mind" is peculiar. There is nothing quite like it elsewhere in the Bible. "Spirit," in this passage, makes sense only if it is taken to mean "attitude" (a very acceptable translation). But what of "renewal"?

Elsewhere in the New Testament, where the word "renewal" appears in English, the Greek word is different from the word used here. In Colossians 3:12 (the parallel passage to this one in Ephesians) and in Romans 12:2, the Greek word used is *anakainoo*, whereas here the word is *ananeoo*. The first Greek word means simply "renewal" (indicating nothing about how the renewal occurs), but the second indicates a special sort of renewal – it is best translated "rejuvenated" (literally, "to make youthful again"). It explains how the renewal takes place.

A youth in those days (before television allowed young people to see all of the hardships of the world) had a childhood. He looked forward to "doing something" in the world. He usually did not become disillusioned and cynical until he was well into his twenties. The youth was ready to accomplish great feats; the world was his oyster!

Here, Paul sets forth the "put off/put on" dynamic for dealing with habit patterns. This dynamic is difficult and requires effort and discipline.[1] Christian counselors soon learn that unless one throws away his cynicism and adopts an

---

1. See my book, *The Christian Counselor's Manual*, for details.

attitude similar to that of the aspiring youth, he will not persevere. So, in the midst of the "put off/put on" verses, Paul intersperses this note on the proper attitude that one must have for the dynamic to take place. It is an attitude that is akin to that which he mentions in I Corinthians 15:58, where he states that one's labor in the Lord is not in vain. For the desired change to occur, there must be an attitude that says that "all the effort is worthwhile."

PHILIPPIANS 2:12

"Work out your own salvation"

So then, my dear friends, just as you have always obeyed before (not only when I am present, but even more so when I am absent), work out your own solution to the problem with fear and trembling.

There has been a variety of explanations of this passage. Contrary to all biblical teaching (e.g., Ephesians 2:8, 9), some have maintained that Paul was teaching that salvation is by works. This is obviously not correct since the letter to Philippians is addressed to "saints" (1:1). He could hardly be telling persons who have been "set apart"[1] to God as His own that they needed to be saved. We can, therefore, dismiss that explanation out of hand.

But, then, what does it mean? Well, there is a considerably larger number of those, whose theology is better, who refer to the passage as an exhortation to sanctification. They may even accompany their explanations of the verse with sayings such as "What God has worked in, you must work out" or "What God has given you in the form of a bud you must bring to flower." These sayings may appeal to some, but they have nothing to do with the passage; they are merely imposed upon it. There is no reason to isolate it from its context in that way.

Well, then, to what *does* the command refer? This is one of those verses which, unlike most of those from the book of Proverbs, depends upon its context for explanation. Notice, the verse opens with the words "So then." The Greek word *oun* ("so then" or "therefore") indicates that the writer is coming to some sort of conclusion. He has been pursuing some point, and what follows is the point itself. So, our con-

---

1. That is the meaning of the word "saint."

cern must be with what Paul has been saying in the preceding context.

Verse 12 is the conclusion to a section that goes back as far as Philippians 1:27. In that verse, with which the section begins, there are statements similar to those found in 2:12. In both places Paul refers to being "absent." As we know, he was writing from prison. In both verses, he also stresses how the Philippian church should live in his absence: "in a manner that is appropriate to the good news about Christ" and "as [they] always obeyed before." Clearly, Paul was concerned that things should go well in his absence. Keeping that in mind, consider the verses intervening between 1:27 and 2:12.[1]

Notice, the emphasis in verses 1:27–30, and all the way through 2:2, is upon unity. I will not discuss the many ways in which Paul addresses the subject in those verses since they are very clear. Obviously, he was much concerned to see to it that the church obey his words so as to become unified, even though he was not on the scene to help bring it about himself. What was the problem? In chapter four we read about a division that had occurred between Euodia and Syntyche, two women who in the past had done much to further the faith.[2] They were now at odds with one another. Presumably, this division was growing and Paul wanted to squelch it as soon as possible.

---

1. Chapter headings, as is frequently true, separate materials that ought not be separated. Read through the passage, ignoring the heading, and notice how it breaks a discussion in two. Neither chapter headings nor verses were in the original biblical writings and are, therefore, not inspired. They were inserted hundreds of years later, not always felicitously. They are truly a convenience in looking up passages, but beyond that often ought to be ignored.

2. Often, the most serious difficulties in congregations occur between those who are the hardest workers. Those on the periphery rarely cause the same sorts of disruptions. They don't have the commitment that would lead them to do so. It is those who are "concerned" to see that things go right (which often means *their way*) who cause splits.

To remedy the situation, Paul stressed the need for unity. How can it be brought about? In Philippians 2:3,4, he sets forth two principles which, if followed, would do so:

1. Consider others better than yourself (v. 3);
2. Be more concerned about the interests of others than about you own (v. 4).

Paul meant that they should concentrate upon ways in which others are truly better than oneself rather than ways in which they are inferior, and that they should have greater concern about furthering the welfare of others than about furthering their own welfare. Clearly, if the Philippians grasped and applied these two principles they would surely achieve greater unity in their church.

Paul then set forth the greatest example of One Who put the interests of others before his own – Jesus Christ. And he called upon the Philippians to have the same attitude about one another as He had toward them (v. 5). In 2:5–11, Paul showed that Jesus, Who existed in the form of God with all of the prerogatives pertaining thereto, was willing to lay these aside[1] in order to save them. He was willing to "humble Himself" by becoming a man, and not only that but a "slave." In addition, he was willing to die for sinners. And, finally, he was willing to die the most shameful death of all – that reserved for the vilest criminals – the death of the cross! He did all of this because He was more concerned about the welfare of others than about His own. *That*, then, is the sort of attitude Paul urged the Philippians to adopt. As a result, Paul pointed out, God rewarded Jesus with the greatest Name of all – "Lord." The God-man now sits as Lord at the Father's right hand. Then, as a conclusion to this discussion concerning the way to unity, comes our verse! How does it fit in?

If that is the sort of attitude the Philippians were to adopt, and that is how God would honor those who do as Jesus did, *then* they would be able to bring unity to the church by

---

1. He "emptied Himself," of these outward manifestations of Deity; not of His Deity itself.

"obeying" what he was writing. This obedience should be forthcoming, just as it always was when Paul was present to direct them. But now, in his absence, they should be all the more careful to obey his instructions. By doing so they would be able to work out their own salvation.

But what does that mean? Simply this: without any hands-on help from Paul the members of the Philippian church should be able to *work out a solution to the problem of disunity on their own.* The is what working out their own salvation means.

The word "salvation" does not always refer to one's eternal salvation. Often, as in the Psalms, the word refers to temporal salvation. One is "saved" from an enemy or from some calamity (cf. Psalm 22:5; 34:6; 59:2; 116:6). The word, in such contexts, means "to rescue" or "to get through some difficulty successfully."

But it is not really necessary to turn to the Psalms or anywhere else to find this use of the word. Paul, himself, had already used it that way in the very letter we are considering. In Philippians 1:19 he wrote that the prayers of the church would result in his "salvation." In saying that, he certainly didn't have eternal salvation in mind. Rather, he was speaking of the trial before Nero in which he would soon plead his cause. He wanted to be sure that during it he would give a faithful witness to the emperor of the world, and thus be "saved" from doing or saying anything that would disgrace his Lord. He was assured that if they prayed for him, the Lord would provide all he needed to boldly exalt Jesus Christ.

So, in 2:12, Paul was telling the Philippians that, without him present, *on their own,* they could work out their own solution to the problem if they obeyed "with fear and trembling." This latter expression means *with great care and concern* so as not to exacerbate problems while trying to solve them.

Then, to bolster their confidence that matters could be dealt with satisfactorily without his help, Paul assures them that they are not really alone: "God is producing in (or among) you both the willingness and the ability to do the things that please Him" (v. 13). God – Whose help is better than Paul's – *was present* to help them reach a proper solution. He would save them from failure.

So, there you have it. There is no need to artificially import extra-contextual sayings to try to explain the passage. A clear, satisfying explanation arises out of a study of the context itself. Perhaps this too is an important lesson to glean from this study: context often answers the questions we have.

I THESSALONIANS 4:16, 17

"we who are alive and remain will be caught up...to meet the Lord in the air"

> The Lord Himself will descend from the sky with an assembling shout, with the voice of the archangel, and with the trumpet of God, and the dead in Christ shall rise first, then we who remain alive shall be caught up together with Him in the clouds as an escort to welcome the Lord as He comes into the air, and so shall we always be with the Lord.

To many, the concept of being "caught up in the clouds" is a difficult concept to understand. That is understandable considering the strange ideas that have come to be associated with it in some circles. The sensational, popular idea that we will be caught up to avoid a great tribulation is not taught in the passage, though it has been proclaimed loudly enough by some teachers. That idea makes no sense, since the dead do not need to be raised in order to escape anything on earth!

"OK," you say, "then why are living and raised Christians caught up?" The question is important and demands a good answer. And there is one forthcoming.

The King James Version here, as in many other passages, created the problems that exist. The translators failed to notice the nuance in the very special term that is used in verse 17. It is not that will be caught up to meet Christ and remain with Him in the air. Exactly not that. The word translated "meet" is used only two other places in the New Testament, once in Matthew 25:6 and in Acts 28:15. In the former passage the shout comes to the wise and foolish virgins, "Here comes the bridegroom; go out and *escort* him back!" The other occasion about which it is used is when Paul was coming to Rome. There we read, "Now the brothers from there, when they heard about us, came as far as the Appian Forum and the Three Taverns to welcome and escort us back."

On both of these occasions, the meeting was a particular kind of meeting. It was a *reception* of someone by those who went to meet him in order to honor him. *Apantesis,* the Greek term associated with these passages and with I Thessalonians 4, is (as Souter in his lexicon says) "almost technical for the reception of a newly arrived official." Notice the virgins escorted the bridegroom back, just as the brothers came out and then escorted Paul back into Rome. The idea is "to meet in order to honor and escort."

The Lord's coming is not our going, but His coming. We will not be caught up to escape anything. Rather, the purpose of going out to meet Him in the air is to honor Him at His coming to earth and to accompany Him back to earth. Whatever one's eschatology, he can prove nothing from this passage other than that this is the appearing of the glory of our great God and Savior, Jesus Christ (Titus 2:13). It is the time of His glory and honor. And it is the time "when He comes to be glorified by His saints and to be admired by all those who have believed" (II Thessalonians 1:10). That is why we are caught up into the air to meet Him – to honor Him as an escort to earth.

I THESSALONIANS 5:22

"Abstain from all appearance of evil"

Abstain from every form of evil.

The problem that many Christians have had with this verse is that they have thought that they must avoid everything that might *appear* to be evil, even when it isn't. I have seen a person avoid drinking from a brown bottle of root beer because, as he put it, "Someone might see me and think that this is a bottle of beer." The issue of whether drinking a bottle of beer is "evil" aside, what he was doing was using I Thessalonians as a guide for avoiding everything others might *think* wrong because it *appeared* so, even when he *knew* that it wasn't so.

It is understandable that those who have been raised on the King James Version of the New Testament might come to this conclusion. However, the passage teaches no such thing. What must be avoided, what one must "abstain" from is evil itself – not some appearance of it. A person may so focus on avoiding appearances of evil that he may lose a true concern about evil. That is a serious problem.

What Paul wrote was that since evil appears in many forms, one must be on his guard for some new manifestation of evil that he may not have been aware of before, and avoid it. After all, unlike truth – which is one – evil may take nearly an infinite number of forms since there are so many ways to go wrong. Its "form" or shape may vary as some new manifestation of evil appears. For instance, in the context (vv. 19–21), which pertains solely to the charismatic age of 30–70 AD (during which miracles such as revelation through prophecy existed[1]), there were problems connected with *false* prophecy. That may be what Paul had in mind. However, he may simply have been stating a broad principle as he sometimes did at the conclusion of a letter. Either way, the principle exists, and has

---

1. For details, see my book, *Signs and Wonders in the Last Days.*

many applications to us today. Some of our major problems are coming in the areas of medical technology, for instance. With the wonders of medical science, many good things appear on the scene; but there are also all sorts of possibilities for evil applications of many of these. We must not simply blunder ahead, assuming that every new "advance" is biblically legitimate. There is a great need for Christians in scientific medicine, together with exegetical theologians, to evaluate these biblically in order to inform the Christian public. Many of the problems that we shall encounter will have to do with life, its meaning and how we must/must not deal with it. As we do so, Paul's principle should alert us to the fact that evil may come in enticing forms.

I Timothy 2:3

"God our Savior, Who wants all men to be saved and come to a knowledge of the truth"

This is good and acceptable before God our Savior, Who wants all sorts of persons to be saved and to come to a full knowledge of the truth.

"How is it," asks someone, "that God wants all men to be saved and, as the Bible makes very plain, many will not be?" The clearer translation in italics, which is from *The Christian Counselor's New Testament*, carries the answer to that question, one that is often raised.

God is not frustrated. His will is ever accomplished. What He wants, He gets. That is certain. In the context, Paul has been telling the men of the congregation that they should pray for "all sorts of persons" (I Timothy 2:1). He then delineates one sample class of persons that he had in mind: "kings and all who are in high positions," a group that they might not have thought to pray for had he not done so.

Then he says that this is good and that God accepts such prayer. Why? Because God wants *all sorts of persons* – even kings and other authorities – to be saved by coming to a full knowledge of the truth. There may have been a prejudice against such persons who may have persecuted Christians and who may have engaged in sinful and oppressive policies. But Paul says that God would accept prayers for them because He wants all kinds of persons, including those in positions of authority, to come to faith in Christ.

Clearly, then, the passage does not speak of an unfulfilled longing that God has for every last person who has ever breathed a breath to be saved. No, that would indeed indicate that God will be frustrated and that His will can be thwarted by men. To the contrary, He intends to save some out of every class of men as an answer to the prayers of believers like Timothy and those in his congregation. And He expects to use them as the human agents by which this occurs.

I TIMOTHY 6:10

"For the love of money is the root of all evil"

> The love of money is a root of all sorts of evils. Some, eager for money, have wandered away from the faith and have pierced themselves through with many sorrows.

On several counts this important verse has proven a stumbling block to many. First, it is often misquoted: "Money is the root of all evil." That is not what Paul wrote. He wrote about the *love* of money, not about money itself. There is no way that the coin of the realm itself could cause any evil of any sort. It is the value that each individual places on money that was in his mind. Those who think that money is the all-important thing in life and "determine to be rich" (I Timothy 6:9) are the ones who do evil. That is not because of money, but because of the *love* of it. All of the commandments have been broken in order to obtain money; men have killed, committed adultery, taken God's Name in vain, and so on – all because they coveted money.

However, this misquotation, in which the word "love" is omitted, is compounded by a further error. The King James Version reads "the root of all evil." The use of the definite article "the" is a poor translation. The indefinite article "a" should be used so that the phrase would correctly read, "*a* root of all sorts of evil." Surely, there are other roots of evil doing besides money, although this erroneous translation seems to say not.

Finally, there is one other problem with the way in which the passage is translated in the 1611 version. The plural "evils" ought to be "all sorts of evils." It is not true either that the love of money is a root of *every* evil. People do evil, all the time, that has nothing to do with money. They get angry because they are proud, they lie because they have been caught in an act of sin, etc. But every *sort* of evil has been committed out of a love for money. People get angry when others' salaries are raised, and their own are not; they lie because they think to do so may be of advantage to them monetarily, and the like.

So, let's understand the verse by properly translating and interpreting it: "the love of money is a root of all sorts of evil."

HEBREWS 6:4–6

"it is impossible to renew again to repentance those who have once been enlightened...if they fall away"

> ...it is impossible to renew again to repentance those who have once been enlightened, who have tasted of the heavenly gift and have become sharers of the Holy Spirit, and have tasted the goodness of God's Word and the miracles of the coming age, if the fall away, because they themselves crucify God's Son all over again and publicly disgrace Him.

This passage, together with its parallel in 10:26–31, has caused much confusion and difficulty to those who have interpreted them as meaning that they might possibly lose their salvation. At first blush, the strong words found in these passages do seem to indicate that this is possible. However, closer examination shows that this is not what the writer of Hebrews was talking about. He had in mind those who had made a false profession of faith, had come under the care and discipline of the church, and had fellowshipped for some time with God's people. Those are the ideas indicated by the words found in 6:4, 5. These good things that they had experienced in the midst of a New Testament congregation were so great that, if they turned their backs on them, denied the faith and left the church, it would be like crucifying Jesus Christ again. There was no more that could be said or done; they already knew the message; there was nothing more to get them to change their mind.

"Well," you say, "How can you be sure of this?" There are, of course, many other passages in the Bible that make it perfectly clear that no true Christian could ever be lost. Elsewhere in this volume I have discussed John 17, where Christ prayed that none would be lost, but all would be one with

Him, in one place, for instance. But it is unnecessary to turn elsewhere to learn that Hebrews 6 was not speaking of a true believer, but of one who had made a false profession of faith.

Look at verses 7 through 9. Here Jesus explains what he had in mind by means of an illustration. Rain falls on two types of ground. One ground yields useful vegetation to a farmer (v. 7) while the other produces nothing but "thorns and thistles." The same message, the same blessings, the same experiences in the midst of a body of God's people falls upon two kinds of people – those who are saved and those who are lost. In time, these things produce two opposite results.

Speaking of the bad ground (i.e., the false professor), the writer says, "we have been convinced of better things about you – things that are true of those who have salvation." So, in this conclusion, he says quite clearly, that he was not speaking of people who are saved. Rather, he was speaking of those who were not.

Doubtless, these are things difficult to understand in Hebrews 6. But one thing is sure – the evidences of apostasy listed in these two places do *not* characterize someone who is truly saved.

HEBREWS 7:3

"Without father or mother or ancestral lineage, without a beginning of days, or end of life"

Now this Melchizedek, king of Salem…without father or mother or ancestral lineage, without a beginning of days or end of life, but like God's Son, he remains a priest perpetually

Could this be true of an individual, some have asked? How is it possible to say such things about anyone other than Adam or Eve? Doesn't everyone since this first pair have all of these? The Gospels even set forth the lineage of Jesus, and as a man, He surely had a beginning of days. What sort of person was Melchizedek anyway?

Well, if you read the passage in Hebrews the way such a questioner does, you will certainly go on being perplexed. But that was not what the writer of the book of Hebrews intended anyone to think. What he is saying about Melchizedek is simply this – the Old Testament account in which he is introduced has him suddenly appearing on the scene without any record of his background. We do not know of his lineage, who his parents were, or any other background. The only thing we have to go on is that he was a priest of God (after a different order than the Levitical priesthood), and that he was also a king of a place called "Salem" (which means "peace" and possibly was the ancient name of Jerusalem). And we know that he was a great person, since Abraham offered tithes to him (Hebrews 7:4).

Moreover, after he appears virtually out of nowhere, in a similar manner he disappears. We know nothing of his demise. He appears, then leaves the record in an equally mysterious manner. Hebrews says that he could be called "King of Righteousness" (the meaning of the name Melchizedek), and that he was King of Salem. In these two senses, he was like our Lord Jesus, Whom Isaiah styled "The Prince of Peace" (Isaiah 9:6) and the "King Who will reign in righteousness" (Isaiah 32:1). And, so far as we can ascertain, since there was no replacement of the Melchizedek priesthood, like our Lord's, his priesthood is "forever." These comparisons show his greatness as a type of Jesus Christ.

So, while not puzzled an longer by his seeming supernatural birth (that was never intended, as we have seen), we ought to be impressed by what we may learn of our Savior through Melchizedek. We shall go on wondering about the things that Hebrews says we do not know about this man until we reach heaven. But we ought not lose sleep over the matter!

HEBREWS 12:17

"he found no place of repentance, though he sought it carefully with tears."

> You know, of course, that afterward when he wanted to inherit the blessing he was rejected. He found no opportunity to change his mind, even though he sought it with tears.

When Esau sold his birthright for a bowl of red bean soup, he made a terrible mistake. Of course, in the providence of God, by which He works all things together for the good of those who love Him, it was a good thing – for Jacob. But for Esau, it turned out, the exchange proved to be nothing more than a hasty, foolish move. It's consequences for him were grave, since the birthright was an important thing in biblical culture. His act was sinful.

"But, could he not repent of his sin?" you ask. Why of course he could. "I thought the passage says that 'he found no place of repentance.' Those words would seem to say that he could *not* repent of his sin."

It is not always proper to translate the original Greek by the English word, "repent." There are passages in which this may lead one astray, as it does in this one. It is better to translate the term into simple English, as I have done in the larger translation above: "He found no opportunity to change his mind." The word "repent" means, simply, "to change the mind."

Now, the real question was, "Did Esau want to change his mind about the way he chose to act, insulting God by treating the birthright blessing in so cavalier manner – or about something else?" That question goes to the heart of the matter. Esau was a "profane" or "godless person" (Hebrews 12:16) who was not at all interested in confessing sin to God. Once his belly was full he came to his senses about what he had done, and changed his mind. He wanted to get his birthright back. But there was no opportunity (or way afforded) for him to do so. He was stuck with the consequences of his decision. Even his tears would not bring it back!

Repentance (*metanoia*, the Greek word used here), we have seen, means "to change the mind." The Old Testament Hebrew word for repentance is *shuv* which means "to turn around." Together, they constitute the full understanding of repentance over sin. Repentance is a change of mind that leads to a change of direction. In Isaiah 55:8, 9, God says that his hearers' ways were not God's ways and that their thoughts were not His thoughts. Repentance deals with both problems: it changes one's ways by changing his thoughts so as to bring both into conformity to God's. There was nothing like that in the heart of Esau who, instead, was like many who whine over the *consequences* of their sins when they cannot change them.

JAMES 5:14–16A

"...anointing him with oil"

> Is anybody among you sick? Let him call for the elders of the church and let them pray over him, rubbing him with oil in the Name of the Lord, and the believing prayer will deliver the one who is sick, and the Lord will raise him up. And if he has committed sins, he will be forgiven. So, confess your sins to one another and pray for one another that you may be healed.

Should the elders of a church still rub seriously sick persons with oil? Because so many don't today, is that why people are not healed? Are we failing them? The answer to both questions is no. The elders ought to visit and pray, but unless one of them is a physician who is treating the sick person, the oil should not be used.

How is that? Well, you see, as my version above indicates, the translation "anoint" is less than accurate. There are two Greek words used in the New Testament for applying oil to a person. One is *chrio*. This important word refers to ceremonial and symbolic acts of applying a liquid (one of which is oil) to the head of another. It is the word from which *Christos* ("Christ"), the "Anointed One" comes. This word is used when one is set apart to a work, and symbolizes his consecration to it.

However, there is another word, which has no symbolic or ceremonial denotation or connotation whatsoever. This word is *aleipho*. This second term is the one used in James 5:14. It is a word that was used for rubbing the body with oil. Wrestlers and other athletes used oil on their bodies.[1] But, in addition, oil was commonly used for medicinal purposes. The New Tes-

---

1. Epictetus writes of an athlete "rubbed down [*aleiphoumenos*] with oil in Bato's wrestling school," Loeb Classical Library, Epictetus, Vol. 2, p. 22.

tament, as well as many other contemporary sources, plainly indicate this.

In Mark 6:13, for instance, we read, "So they went out and preached that people must repent, and they cast out many demons, and they rubbed oil on many sick people and healed them." Clearly, part of the task of the Twelve on this mission was to heal as well as preach. They did much the same thing as James recommends in his letter. The good Samaritan also engaged in first aid, which involved the pouring of oil on the victim's wounds: "So he went over to him, bound up his wounds and poured oil and wine on them" (Luke 10:34). Isaiah refers to Israel's pitiful spiritual condition under the metaphor of one who's terrible physical straits are as follows:

> The whole head is sick and the whole heart is faint. From the sole of the foot even to the head there is nothing sound in it, only bruises, welts and raw wounds, not pressed out or bandaged, nor softened with oil (Isaiah 1:5^b, 6).

This verse even suggests how the oil was used medicinally. Oil was poured on the wound and rubbed into the swelling. It may also be presumed that, when they were available, medicinal herbs would be mixed with the oil base.

Extra-biblical sources attest to these things as standard treatment. Galen, the physician, speaks of "medicated oil" in his *Methedo* 11:16, and Hippocrates, like Jesus, refers to "smearing oil and wine."[1] Hippocrates, like Isaiah, also speaks of applying a dissolved "black drug, putting linen on it [the wound] and moisten[ing] it with oil."[2] Dr. E.T. Withington, himself a physician like Hippocrates, wrote in the introduction of the Loeb Classical Library volume just cited, "The under-bandages and the folded pieces of linen called *splenees* (pads or compresses) were usually soaked in some application" He goes on to mention the use of "cerate...wax lique-

---

1. *Aleiphas elaio kai oino* (in A.T. Robertson, *Luke the Historian*, [Baker], 1977, p. 97).
2. In the Loeb Classical Library, *Hippocrates*, Vol. 3, p. 35.

fied in olive oil or oil of roses, supposed to prevent inflammation...wine and oil were also used."[1]

Non-medicinal uses also make it clear that *aleipho* meant to rub or smear a substance. For instance, Dio Chrysostom, quoting Diogenes, tells of people from Pontus who used to smear (*aleiphes*) themselves with "the lard of pigs." That is about as unceremonial as an act could be!

Clearly, it was a normal practice among the Jews to apply unguents, oil and the like, in much the same way a person today would apply makeup. The Septuagint (the Greek translation of the Old Testament) gives unmistakable evidence of this in such passages as Ruth 3:3; II Samuel 12:20, 14:2; II Chronicles 28:15; Esther 2:12. And, in the Septuagint of Ezekiel *aleipho* is regularly used to describe the "plastering" of a wall (Ezekiel 13:10, 11, 12, 14, 15)! It should be evident, then, that what James is talking about is using medicine prayerfully. In a context referring to sickness, that seems certain.

The elders applied medicine (as did the Samaritan on the Jericho road) because there was not a doctor's office on every corner or telephones that could be used to call 911. Even with the relatively small number of physicians available, there must have been many who preferred home remedies. There was no certifying body like there is today that could wield power to keep people from practicing medicine without a "license." Consequently, anyone could prescribe (as Paul did when writing to Timothy: I Timothy 5:23). The elders, then, would not have been amiss in using the common healing methods of the day, together with prayer. The key in the passage is that the medication is not used alone; it was consecrated by prayer.

What ought to be retained in the passage is not merely the idea of using medicine and prayer, but the practice of asking the sick person (if there seems to be some reason for doing so) whether he has brought the sickness upon himself by means

---

1. Loeb, pp. xx, xxi.

of some sin which he needs to confess. The "if" is important. Not all illness stems from personal sin, but the passage assumes that some does (perhaps more than we recognize).

Note, also, calling for the elders was the responsibility of the sick person. They are not required to "discover" the fact that he is ill; the "grapevine" often works too slowly for that. And they should not be summoned for every small illness. Note that they are to "pray *over*" the sick Christian who has called for them. This presumes that he is lying upon a bed of sickness, or at best, confined to a chair.

All in all, it should be plain to those who study it carefully that the passage is quite sensible. Prayer is required, but the normal means of using medication is also encouraged. There is nothing here for those sects who use the passage in a nearly magical manner, expecting God to do miracles by means of some "anointing oil."

To sum up, look at the facts:

1. The core of the context is sickness. That, in itself, ought to lean one toward the medicinal view.

2. Of two words available to him that are used in the Bible, James chose the one that is non-ceremonial.

3. This non-ceremonial term is used of smearing, rubbing down, plastering and applying unguents.

4. The word is regularly used in and out of Scripture to describe the application of oil as a medicine.

JAMES 5:19, 20

"The one who brings back a sinner...
will save him from death"

> My brothers, if anybody among you errs from
> the truth and somebody brings him back, you
> should know that the one who brings back a
> sinner from the error of his way will save his
> soul from death and will cover a lot of sins.

The major problem in these two verses is whether or not
the passage is evangelistic. The saving one from "death" could
mean one of two things:

1. Eternal death in hell. If his meaning is true, then the verse
   must be interpreted as meaning that bringing the wan-
   derer back from the error of his ways is to cover a lot of
   sins by the forgiveness that he receives in Jesus Christ at
   salvation. Doubtless, whenever there is the conversion of
   a lost person, many sins are "covered" by the blood of
   Jesus Christ. The word "cover" is the Old Testament word
   for forgiveness, a term that is quite appropriate for James,
   who was writing to a congregations of Jewish converts in
   the "dispersion."[1]

2. The passage, on the other hand, may be speaking of physical death. This is the more difficult interpretation. Nev-
   ertheless it is the true one. It seems clear that James ends
   his letter with a strong exhortation to retrieve those sheep
   who have been wandering from Christ's fold and thereby
   cover (reduce the number of, or keep from bringing up)
   their sins. The reason to opt for this understanding is that
   in verse 19 the person who is brought back from the
   errors of his way is said to be "anybody among you."

---

1. Jews spread out over the Mediterranean world, but not living in Palestine.

That seems clearly to indicate that he is one of the "brothers" who are being addressed in that verse.

This brother, who has wandered from the truth, may have become involved in activities that would lead to physical death. Although that is not the preferred understanding, since it is not likely to happen to all who do so. Rather, the death in view may be the judgment of God within the Church of God, about which we read in I Corinthians 11:30. There, those who "sleep" are believers who have been misusing the Lord's supper as a time to feast, get drunk, etc., and, thereby fail to "discern" the Lord's body (v. 29). That is to say, they miss the whole point of the Lord's Supper: to show forth Christ's death.

We do not know the "error" into which those to whom James was writing might have fallen – or whether, indeed, there was some particular error at all. Perhaps it was but a general warning about what was possible that he had in mind – but we do know that it had to do with physical, rather that spiritual, death because James was speaking of an erring *believer*. However, it would seem that James must have had something quite serious in mind.

There are some commentators who think that the sins that are covered are those of the one who brings back the wandering brother. This cannot be true since it would amount to forgiveness of sins by works. It would seem, rather, that James still has in mind situations like those mentioned in verses 15 and 16 where a brother has become sick enough to be bedridden (and possibly dying) because of his sin. The passages are surely connected. It is to be remembered, however, not all sickness is the result of sin (notice the "if" in v. 15). But, clearly some is. It is, therefore, only right to suppose that James is continuing this thought when he warns against possible death as the result of sin. Erring believers, who had not yet been judged, might be raised from a deathbed by the prayers of faithful brothers, and brought back to the path of righteousness before judgment came upon them. And, in the process, many sins that had been committed, would no longer become a slanderer or gossip among the members of the church.

Proverbs 10:12, which is the source from which James obtained his proposition, refers to "love" covering sins. Surely, one of the ways in which a believer may show love to another is to rescue him from his error, thereby helping him avoid God's judgment brought upon him because of it. In the Proverbs passage, the contrasting line of the verse is, "Hatred stirs up strife." The contrast between that and "love covers all sorts of transgressions," seems to be that, rather than exposing a person's sins in such a way that it causes trouble for him and God's people, in love (rather than hatred) one should calm the situation by covering those sins. The covering, in the exposition by James, takes place by restoring an erring brother (cf. Galatians 6:1) rather than "stirring up" more trouble for him. The verse, as does its source in Proverbs, calls for love toward one's brother – even when he is involved in serious sin.

I PETER 3:18, 19

"By Whom also He preached to the spirits who are in prison"

…being put to death in the flesh but made alive by the Spirit, by Whom also He went and preached to the spirits who are in prison.

Will there be a second chance after death for those who did not trust Christ while here on earth, an opportunity to hear and believe the gospel preached from His own lips? That is what some interpreters of the passage think. But in Hebrews 9:27 we are clearly told, "It is appointed to man once to die, and after that the judgment." There is certainly no second chance.

Well, then what do these words mean? Did Christ after His death preach to the disembodied spirits of men? If not to give them a second chance, then what? The answer is that He did *not* preach to spirits in prison after His death. The passage is speaking about the days of Noah (v. 20) and the years during which he patiently waited while building his ark and preaching to men who would not believe. What Peter is saying is that these unbelievers are in prison *now* because *then –*
in the days of Noah – they "disobeyed[1] the Word." But what of Christ's preaching? Jesus preached to those who are now in prison *during the days of Noah*. He went by the Spirit, we are informed, and preached to them through Noah. That is the import of the passage. It was to warn that there would be no second chance that Peter wrote this passage: when one disobeys in this life, there is nothing left in the afterlife but the prison of hell. Peter is warning his readers to be sure that they believe, so that after death they will not suffer the same fate as these spirits.

But what of the rest of the passage (vv. 20–22)? That too is perplexing. Yes, and a bit more difficult to understand. But we

---

1. Peter's term for unbelief.

will attempt to make it clear. He says that eight persons – Noah and his wife, along with his three sons and their wives – were "saved by water." The water of the flood destroyed all others, but the very same water that destroyed others "saved" them. Now, that is the first thing that is essential to see.

Next, note that our baptism corresponds to this "salvation." Peter makes it clear that he is not speaking of water baptism ("not by the removal of grime from the flesh"). The only other baptism of which the New Testament knows anything is the baptism of the Spirit (I Corinthians 12:13). So, it is the baptism of the Spirit to which Peter refers. This baptism, he says, involves an appeal to God for a good conscience. If water baptism saved, we would be saved by a ceremony rather than by the grace of God through faith. No, it is Spirit baptism that is in view.

How does Spirit baptism save? Peter says, "by the resurrection of Christ" (v. 21). As the ark raised the eight from destruction so, too, Christians are raised above eternal destruction by being baptized into Jesus Christ (cf. Romans 6:1ff) and are, thereby, saved. It is our resurrection with Christ (v. 21) that raises us above destruction. We are saved by virtue of being in Him.

The "appeal" to God for a good conscience refers to requesting from God a good conscience through the purifying work of the Holy Spirit Who, when He enters into our lives, cleanses us from sin and unites us to Christ. When we are counted to be "in Christ" through Spirit baptism (union with Him), we are reckoned to have experienced all that He did, including His resurrection. So we are "saved" by being raised *in* Him as those *in* the ark were saved by being raised above destruction.

II PETER 3:9

"Not willing that any should perish, but that all should come to repentance"

The Lord is not delaying His promise in the sense that some think of delay, but He is patiently waiting for you, not wanting any of you to be destroyed, but everyone to come to repentance.

If He doesn't want any to perish, then why do some perish? Cannot God do as He pleases? Has man got God stymied? Obviously all do not come to repentance; how then is it that God's will is frustrated – or is it? Those are the sorts of questions that have been raised over these words in II Peter.

The problem is that the verse has been considered out of its context. Let's ask the question, "Who are the 'any' referred to in the verse?" And for that matter, "Who are the 'all'?" The correct answer to those questions is the answer to the problem.

In the passage, Peter is talking about scoffers who will ask "What happened to the promise of His coming?" (v. 4), referring to the second coming of Jesus Christ. He reminds them that God, by His Word, formed the world and then destroyed it with a flood. By that same Word of promise He will come and will judge and destroy ungodly men (vv. 5–7). Moreover, he says, time with God is not the same as it is with man (v. 8). Then comes our verse.

In the light of the context, here is what Peter was saying: "God hasn't delayed His promise," in the sense that these scoffers have in mind. They think that He has either changed His mind or has forgotten it. Rather, Peter says, He is "patiently waiting" (v. 8). Waiting for what? For "you," he says. God is waiting for every one who will ever be saved to come to repentance. He wants none of them to perish, so He is waiting until the last one of His elect shall come to repentance. The "any" and the "all," then, refer to any of *you* and all of *you* believers. God will not bring about the destruction of the present defiled world until the very last Christian has been born and come to faith in Christ. Taken in context, the passage makes sense. Rather than God's will being frustrated, it asserts that it will be fulfilled to the fullest!

I JOHN 2:2

"And he is the propitiation for our sins:
and not for ours only, but also
for the sins of the whole world."

…if anybody sins, we have an Advocate Who
stands face to face with the Father – Jesus
Christ, the Righteous One. He Himself is the
appeasing sacrifice for our sins, and not ours
only, but also for those of the whole world.

The King James Version says that Jesus is the propitiation
for our sins. My translation above makes the word clearer: a
propitiation is a sacrifice that appeases God's wrath. As the old
writers used to put it, it smooths out God's wrinkled brow.
His anger is removed, and the relationship that was marred
by sin is now reestablished as it was in Adam before the fall.

"But the whole world is not in a proper relationship to
God, is it? Christ's death does not remove God's anger from
all persons. Some continue under His wrath all of the way to
death and hell" (John 3:36).

You are right.

"Then, how does this verse apply? It says that Christ's sacrificial death removed God's anger from everyone in the
world, doesn't it?"

No, it does not.

"Well, does His sacrificial death *potentially* remove His
anger so that when one believes it actually happens?"

No, that isn't right either. The verse says that God was
propitiated for "those of the whole world." It says nothing
about a potential sacrifice. Either Christ's death smoothed
God's brow in reference to those for whom He died, or the
verse is wrong.

"Well, then, how can the fact that men and women will go
to hell be squared with this verse?"

That, of course, is why the verse is being considered in this book. You see, John constantly contrasts the Jews with the whole world throughout his books. He is concerned to let the reader know that salvation is not for Jews alone. What he is saying, then, is that Jesus' death was a propitiation for people from all the world, not for "ours [Jews] only." The universality in the verse has to do with the contrast that he sets up in those words "ours only" versus "the whole world."

If Christ's death were only potentially efficacious, it would be insufficient. What He did, actually satisfied God so that He would no longer have anger toward (and ultimately pour out wrath upon) those for whom Christ died. It was an appeasing sacrifice; by it God truly was appeased. All ideas of potentiality are foreign to the text and actually amount to saying that what Christ did was not effective, but was only potentially so. What would make the difference is that *we* would have to add something to it in order to make it effective. That is utterly wrong; it makes salvation at least partly by our works and is demeaning to the Savior.

I JOHN 3:9

"and he can't go on sinning because he has been born of God"

Whoever has been born of God isn't committing sin because His seed remains in him, and he can't go on sinning because he has been born of God.

Does a believer sin? Is perfection in this life possible? This verse raises such questions in the thinking Christian's mind. It may even lead him to question his salvation. "If a Christian cannot go on sinning," he may reason, "then I must not be a Christian because I still sin."

First of all, we know that the verse cannot mean that anyone can be perfect in this life because of what John says elsewhere in this letter: "If we say that we don't have any sin, we deceive ourselves and the Truth isn't in us" (I John 1:8; cf. also 1:10). These words are plain enough. So there must be another explanation of our problem verse.

And there is. The idea that someone can't do... something admits of at least two interpretations:

1. It is *impossible* for him to perform that act (this is the interpretation that causes the trouble).

2. It is *inconsistent* for him to perform that act (this interpretation meets all requirements, makes good sense, and causes no difficulty).

To say that a person *can't* do something, while meaning that it is it is not consistent for him to do it under certain circumstances, is a valid interpretation of the verse. It corresponds admirably with a passage such as Mark 2:19, where we are told that the children of the bridegroom "can't fast" while the bridegroom is present. Of course, they were *able* to do so – what Jesus was saying is that it would be *unthinkable* or *out of character* for them to do it under those conditions.

So, too, it is unthinkable, out of character, for the one who possesses the seed of God within Him to go on sinning as if it were not true, as if no change had ever occurred in his life. But because He *has* been born of God – has God as His Father, and thus carries His character traits (seed) within him – it is out of character for him to go on sinning.

I JOHN 5:14–17

"A sin unto death"

> This is the boldness that we have before Him:
> that if we ask anything according to His will,
> He listens to us. Since we know that He listens
> to us whatever we may ask, then we know that
> we shall have whatever we ask from Him. If
> anybody sees his brother committing a sin that
> doesn't lead to death, he shall ask and He will
> give life to him (that is, to those committing a
> sin that doesn't lead to death). There is a sin
> that leads to death; I don't say that you should
> inquire about that. All unrighteousness is sin,
> but there is a sin that doesn't lead to death.

In these verses there are at least two problems that need to
be addressed. One has to do with the idea that there are sins
that lead to death and there are sins that don't lead to death.
To what is the apostle referring? The other problem is the
common interpretation that one should not ask God for life of
the person who has committed a sin that leads to death.

Let's consider the second problem first. Should we not
pray for our brothers in all circumstances? John seems to say
"No. There is one circumstance in which you must not do so."
How shall we understand this?

Notice, I have translated the end of verse 16 differently
from the way that some others have. Those who translate
"ask for," "make request for this" or "pray about that" con-
fuse the reader by this rendering. Let me try to clear things
up. In the translation from *The Christian Counselor's New
Testament* at the head of this page, I have translated the words
in question this way: "I don't say that you should *inquire
about* that." The words "inquire about" (or "ask about") are
key to the understanding of John's words.

In the original Greek there are two different words. One,
aiteo, means "to ask *for*" or "pray." That is the word used in

the earlier part of verse 16, when John writes, "he shall ask and He will give life to him." But in the words referring to a brother who has committed a sin leading toward death, the word is *eratao*. This second word does not refer to prayer at all. It means "to inquire *about*, to ask *about*."[1] Instead of prayer, John is referring to inquisitiveness. He did not want Christians inquiring into the details of another's sin. Too often, this happens, and when it does, more often than not, that leads to gossip. So it seems clear that John did not want Christians prying into details concerning the sinful activities of others.

That clears up one problem; what about the other? What does John mean when he speaks of a "sin that leads to death?" Plainly, we can say that John is not talking about apostasy from the faith as some have thought. How do we know that? Because John calls the one who commits the sin leading to death a "brother" (v. 16). So that idea may be dismissed at the outset.

Then to what does he refer? Well, first, notice that John contrasts two kinds of sins: the sin that does not lead to death and the one that does. In the passage, he is explaining that when we ask God for something according to His will He will grant it (vv. 14, 15). That means we may be bold in our prayers.[2] Christians should not cringe as they come before His throne of Grace. However, there are limits to this boldness. We may go so far and no farther. When a Christian "sees his brother committing a sin that doesn't lead to death" he may ask for God to give him life and expect an answer. But if a brother commits a sin that does lead to death, the implication is that when an answer does not come others must not

---

1. Sometimes the distinction between the two words has to do with one who is superior speaking to one who is inferior and the other way around. That does not seem to be the distinction in view here.

2. The word for boldness is not the one that means "daring activity." Rather, *parresia* refers to bold speech. It is speech that is straightforward without hedging what one says for fear of consequences. God wants us to pray before Him that way.

expend their efforts to determine why, or to find out the details about why God hasn't answered. He is to leave the matter there – in God's hands.

So, then, what is the sin that leads to death? Since spiritual death is not in view, John must be thinking of physical death. As "life" and "death" refer to *physical* life and death in the earlier part of verse 16 when John refers to praying for the brother who has not committed a sin that leads to death,[1] so here, too, the word "death" must also refer to physical life and death. The sin that leads to death may refer to crimes that require capital punishment or, less likely, to those sins that God punishes with death (cf. I Corinthians 11:30). Paul once referred to his willingness to submit willingly to capital punishment if he were guilty of being charged with it (Acts 25:11).

John is interested in putting down curiosity and gossip on the part of believers. If there is any talk at all it is to be to God. This is, therefore, a powerful passage to use in restraining idle curiosity about why God does not always answer the prayers of believers for one another when they have committed sins.

---

1. It would make no sense to refer these words to eternal life and death.